FIRE MOUNTAIN

A Nation's Heritage in Jeopardy

FIRE MOUNTAIN

A Nation's Heritage in Jeopardy

by *William K. Medlin*

SUNSTONE
PRESS

SANTA FE
New Mexico

First Edition

Printed in the United States of America

Library of Congress Cataloging in Publication Data:

Medlin, William K.
    Fire mountain: a nation's heritage in jeopardy / by William K. Medlin
        p.   cm
    Includes bibliographical references.
    ISBN 0-86534-228-8 (pbk.)
    1. Lassen Volcanic National Park (Calif.)–History. 2. Indians of North America–California–Lassen Volcanic National Park–History. 3. Landscape assessment–California–Lassen Volcanic National Park–History. 4. Geographical perception–California–Lassen Volcanic National Park–History. I. Title.
    F868.L34M44   1996
    979.4'24–dc20   95-31587
                                              CIP

Published by SUNSTONE PRESS
        Post Office Box 2321
        Santa Fe, NM 87504-2321 / USA
        (505) 988-4418 / orders only (800) 243-5644
        FAX (505) 988-1025

TABLE OF CONTENTS

LIST OF FIGURES

ACKNOWLEDGEMENTS

The author's debt has accumulated over many years to many individuals who have contributed to the conception, implementation, and finally to the results of a project that turned out to be this book. Originally, back in 1987, I volunteered to do a history of Lassen Volcanic National Park for the National Park Service (NPS). The dimensions of the task, to be done properly and professionally, were immense. Nonetheless, after almost four years of labor on a part-time basis, the job was done. The volume lies on the shelf in the Office of the Western Region of NPS, gathering dust, because the wheels of bureaucracy designed to process the public's interests are bogged down in red tape.

Special thanks go to Park Naturalists Ellis Richard and Richard Vance, whose enthusiasm and support in this enterprise were initially deeply appreciated. Thanks go out to the day-to-day "sluggers," employees like Nancy Bailey who helped me find useful information in masses of paper, and to Gertrude Rutledge whose fantastic memory and thorough knowledge of the park files saved me tons of time in searching for the right data. Career officers, like Rangers Larry Feser and retiree Les Bodine, were most generous of their time in supplying personal knowledge never recorded in official memoranda or reports. Lassen's current Park Naturalist, Betty Knight, provided access to photographs which are invaluable.

I wish I could thank Lynne Walker Collins, Lassen's first superintendent, and members of his family, whom I tried to contact but was unsuccessful in doing so. Collins' detailed record-keeping of his early years and his great dedication to the Lands of Lassen which he loved so much, were inspiring to me as I plodded through the reams of reports compiled on just this one national park. His sore sacrifice at the hands of brutal political bureaucrats remains a black blemish on NPS administration and contains a lesson for all of us who care for fairness and justice in our democratic polity. I also wish I could thank Ishi, the last of the Yana-Yahi people, for leaving with us so much of their rich cultural heritage.

There are many, many persons to whom I am indebted whose mention would fill many pages. I wish to thank in particular my daughter, Nancy Christine Medlin, who served as a park naturalist at Lassen and many other of America's beautiful preserves. Her deep commitment to a wholesome environment for her family and her nation, as well as her detailed knowledge of Lassen Park, were constant inspirations to me. I also want to thank my wife, Betty, for her willingness to read and criticize my prose, which reflects the somewhat stilted style of a teacher writing instructions for a class on the theory of planning! Although her native tongue is French, she has a special feel for what is readable. Accolades could go on and on, but I shall stop here. For those not mentioned personally, you will understand why, and I deeply thank you for that.

PREFACE

In northeastern California prior to 1800, Native Americans had lived in and been nurtured by the mountain wilderness for thousands of years. Their life styles had made no noticeable impacts on land, forest or water, which remained in a pure state of nature. During the last half of the nineteenth century, however, the arrival of white settlers brought in its wake almost immediate degradation of the wilderness environment. At the expense of the Native American tribes and cultures, the new occupiers of the land set out to exploit its resources with no regard for the future. But during the twentieth century, the American Government has sought to halt degradation and to preserve, even restore, some of this wilderness by creating a national park under public management.

This book traces events giving rise to conflicts over this mountain region, which we call the "Lands of Lassen." The main and highest peak was named for a European emigrant, Peter Lassen. Some local Indian tribes referred to Lassen Peak as the Fire Mountain, because it is a volcano which over the millenia has spewed flames and fiery lava from its crater. Other tribal folks named it Snow Mountain because its peak is snow-covered most of the year. In hindsight, we might refer to the area as the "Lands of Ishi," the name of the last known survivor of his Yana-Yahi tribe inhabiting the area. Ishi, whose fate will be discussed in detail in Chapter 2, miraculously carried the spirit of his ancestors and their culture into the twentieth century. While his people saw themselves as being one with nature, the European-American settlers saw nature primarily as a resource for their materialistic life-styles. Deeply imbedded conflicts have emerged from this dichotomy.

This book raises an issue: What kind of relationship between the human being and nature will best serve the interests of both? The Native American had defined this relationship in one way and the white American in another. These divergencies have impacted on the entire history of the American preservation and conservation movement. They beg for attention in terms of public policy, citizens' attitudes toward national parks and wilderness, and the day-to-day management of our public domains.

As a youngster I spent most of my summers in Lassen's forests and along the streams of Mill Creek and Deer Creek, both bordering on aboriginal Yana-Yahi tribal territory. Rugged features of this volcanic and glacial region were softened by gentle, lush meadows, placid lakes and graceful valleys, much like other Cascade mountains to the north, of which Fire Mountain was the southernmost. Rainbow trout and "Dolly Vardens," a western brook trout, were plentiful in the cold waters of the streams we fished. Deer, chipmunks, eagles, falcons, and many other mountain creatures were common companions as my brother and I trespassed their native habitats. This pleasant but also foreboding country, sometimes referred to as "those happy grounds," still had an idyllic aura about it even though settlers of European origin had homesteaded there for over seventy-five years.

These "Lands of Ishi" with their markedly alpine features reflect glacial sculpturing which, between ten and twenty thousand years ago, carved valleys, canyons, cirques, and other land forms that give the some four hundred square miles surrounding the peak itself a unique character. Together with the effects of volcanic action, these glacial features display a fascinating geological panorama dating back tens of millions of years.

The time was the 1930s, and little did I realize that the scenes which I took for granted still resembled closely those where seventy years or so previously the native tribal groups and clans had made their homes. In the interim they had almost totally disappeared from the region as the occupation of their ancient lands by white settlers spread. The people of the Yahi Indian man, Ishi, had vanished.

Nothing I saw around me could have been identified as native or aboriginal, recalling their former cultural presence there, which had spanned several thousand years. In fact, it seemed they had come and gone without leaving a visible trace, no buildings, no roads, no monuments. And I did not know what an "Indian" was, except for the distorted images I got from the Saturday matinee cowboy-and-Indian movies. Yet, I somehow sensed that humans had not yet spoiled these lands. I felt a certain harmony, balance, and unity in nature which became a part of me. Natural things had their unique characters and built-in relationships to each other, to which I could add nothing. With patience and experience, I learned a little about how nature works, or in Norman Maclean's words, how "to think like a fish."

What had, in fact, changed dramatically over those two generations was the role which a new breed of human beings intended to exert through their interactions with that natural endowment. My use of Lassen's resources was simple, innocent and care free: recreation and leisure, uninhibited by either nature or man. In that seventy-five year interval, the new humans had begun to make different demands on the region whose implications would, in time, threaten both natural and cultural resources in the area. They built structures, cleared forests, bulldozed roads, and ranged livestock everywhere. Later in life I learned that the implications of these transformations stood diametrically opposed to the relationships which aboriginal cultures had maintained in the same region for millenia.

My ignorance of both the natural and cultural past of Fire Mountain was exposed in raw form one day in the village of Mineral, a few miles from Lassen National Park. I noticed a strange-looking man enter the general store. He was dark, short and heavy, and wore a pony tail under a round, flat hat. "Who's that?" I asked my dad. With a slight tinge of derision in his voice he replied, "Oh, he's just an Indian from those Hat Creek people." I had never seen a "live" Native American. There were so few around, to be sure. Still, my father's reply meant very little to me and I forgot the incident until some fifty years later. So much for a young American's awareness of his social and cultural heritage at the time.

The story in this book, then, is about the reflection, onto nature's unspoiled tapestries, of varying attitudes held by human predators toward this small corner of America's original landscape. Original here means that which nature itself presents to the eye, untrammeled by human designs and technologies. It includes those changes wrought by nature upon itself, through endless workings of natural forces and ecological adaptations, like the swirls of a river that create underwater chambers for trout. It refers to the unblemished, the pure, the undefiled. Seen in this light, it becomes a story of humans' predations on their own vital inheritance, on the original web of life which sustains all creatures and living things. The story also explores in a major way our nation's efforts to redeem the past, to empower politicians to redesign land use and to chart a new set of relationships between human beings and the natural world.

But what was to be redeemed, and how best to go about the process of reclaiming our heritage and preserving priceless legacies of both natural and cultural value? The answers to this and related questions came from a diversity of interests, perspectives, goals and methods. They came from those in government entrusted with national and state preserves, from the users of the national park and its environs and from entrepreneurs who sought to make economic gain from the area's resources. The absence of any organized Native American representation created a dependency on whites' "good will" in finding a place for the lost cultures in any restorative efforts. We must also recognize that there were interests stemming from political influences seeking advantage by supporting one or the other partisan group. That these many interests would drift into collision courses with each other, as well as run parallel to each other on certain issues, is no doubt typical of human institutions vying for influence and control over resources. We humans have created a political world which overlays the natural one. Herein lies a profound dilemma for humankind's ability to safeguard this earth for future generations.

This story winds through a number of episodes which test human understanding of nature, man's relation thereto and human ingenuity to avoid its undoing. It explores society's custodianship of and means for managing the natural environment, defined as a national park. Archeological and anthropological studies, research in the life sciences as well as geological surveys, scrutiny of management plans and first-hand observations of park operations are all resources and methods I used to produce the needed data for writing this fascinating, but tragic story.

Love and care for natural beauty is a cultural, not a human, attribute; it needs be developed humanly. One of the greatest admirers and promoters of parks-for-people expressed his commitment to that ideal as follows:

> "... look up through the crown of these trees into
> the sky. Not in this life, not even in a great
> cathedral, will you feel closer to your Maker. For
> men built the cathedral, but God created the trees.
> And I am sure He created them for people – all the
> people of our country and our earth …. And I
> think the best way to make sure that these trees
> remain forever the property of the people is to
> get them into the parks." (Conrad Wirth)

Can one contest this artful statement? Perhaps not, but the question of how the people use the park preserves is one which has divided and continues to divide society. It seems fair to say that the public at large which supports the national park through taxation should decide that question. If the decision rests on good, sound, and reliable information, then we might hope that the future of these domains may rest secure. Our journey here will help tell us how well informed these decisions and their defenders have been.

Homo sapiens has never stood, and does not now stand, alone in this universe, although his ego and conceit often defy this truth. Philosophers as well as biologists have joined their voices in affirming the infinite webs connecting all life. We ignore these webs at our own peril. This theme is a thread running throughout this story whence the last Stone Age man, Ishi, finally surrendered to white domination in 1911.

The reader is invited to trace this thread and, weighing the evidence scattered across its pages, to decide whether the story is telling the truth. According to Ishi, if one truly understands nature, one will be able to know the truth.

It is in the spirit of this simple but profound observation that this volume is offered as a contribution to the storehouse of Americana.

— William K. Medlin
Albuquerque
July/1994

13

CHAPTER 1

FIRE MOUNTAIN: NATURAL AND CULTURAL HERITAGE

As mentioned earlier, when the Dane, Peter Lassen, gave his family name to Mount Lassen, the Native Americans inhabiting the area had known it for centuries as Fire Mountain, the Yana-Yahi name, and as Snow Mountain, from the Maidu. By both personal experience and oral tradition, they knew its fiery history. Their intuition also told them that this mountain range had its origins in turbid volcanic activity. By their naked eye they could also tell that some of the peaks surrounding Lassen itself, the highest one, had been broken, sheared or split by massive forces. This was their geology, knowledge gleaned from natural observation. Because its volcanic flames and boiling springs have been its most prominent features, we choose to adopt the Yana-Yahi name, Fire Mountain, for this story.

Modern geology classifies this mountain range as part of the earth-girdling "Ring of Fire" which encircles the Pacific Ocean's rim. It occupies the southern-most tier of the Cascade Mountains, ranging from British Columbia into North-ern California. Like others in this volcanic chain, Lassen Peak and those adjacent to it were created by powerful earth-building forces which have been at work for tens of millions of years. Dating back at least 30-40 million years, these forces were produced by oceanic and continental plates in motion and collision, causing massive ridges to rise, forming mountain chains, generating intense heat beneath the earth's surface and melting rock into volcanic lava. This lava tended to rise to the surface through vents piercing the earth's crust, thus forming new peaks and other mountain forms. The Cascade Range is a classic example of these tremendous earth-moving forces. Thousands of years ago the first humans, Native Americans, made their homes in this mountainous environment and developed cultures that endured until the last quarter of the 19th century.

While the Cascade Range was formed over the last million years, its volcanic rocks date back some fifteen million years, when the present landscapes were in their early stages of development. The outcomes of this long process, which dominate the Lassen region, are a series of volcanic peaks which give the area its prime characteristics. A special and unusual volcanic form lies next to Lassen and is known as Cinder Cone. This conically shaped accumulation of ash is the most recent volcanic formation in the region and was last known to be active during 1850-51.

Aside from towering Lassen Peak itself (almost 11,000 feet), the most prominent physical feature of the entire range is the remains of a once huge volcano, Tehama. Spanning about fifteen miles at its base, and rising to a height of over 11,000 feet, Mount Tehama lay astride deep faults. In time these faults caused the mountain to collapse into a huge caldera, or basin. This depression left a series of broken mountain peaks around the rim of the caldera and canyons separated by rugged ridges. Thereafter, a new vent for fiery lava to rise developed on Tehama's east side, which ultimately became Lassen Peak, an accumulation of molten lava and rock. Its creation appears to have been completed about 5,000 years ago, except for occasional, intermittent spewing of lava as occurred during 1914-15. In geological time, Lassen is a comparatively recent mountain formation. (For details, see Notes.)

The whole Lassen region presents a fascinating display of earth-building activities which continue to bring about changes in the range's features. While the huge glaciers of the last Ice Age, which gouged out canyons and meadows, have long since melted, many rushing streams continue year-round to erode the slopes and canyons. Gale force winds, avalanches, rock slides and, over the past century, human activity constantly work changes upon the varied landscapes. Hundreds of hot springs, fumaroles and geysers also continuously impact the natural heritage created by the Tehama and Fire Mountain volcanoes.

These monumental and complex forces created a mosaic of landscape designs bearing many different descriptions: multi-colored dunes, vast treeless slopes, emerald lakes, thick coniferous forests, vaulting crags, rugged canyons and gorges, lush meadows, snow-blanketed peaks and ridges, and still other features. For millenia a wide range of living organisms have thrived here, including human beings. Above 8,000 feet vegetation is sparse, while the range of 5,000 to over 7,000 feet harbors forests with abundant wild life, water and other sources of life.

At the outer edges of the range, in those lower elevations where foothills dominate, semi-arid conditions prevail during most of the year. This has limited tree growth and other vegetation available for food. Stands of pin oak and "digger" pine predominate in this lower zone, followed by chaparral with its manzanita thickets Beyond this region and toward the valley floor on the west slope, the terrain sinks to only a few hundred feet above sea level. Sparse rainfall during nine months of the year renders most of the lower-level foothills and valley floor desert-like and barren in appearance, with limited food resources except during springtime and along the rivers.

At higher elevatons, from 4,000 to 6,000 feet, glacially carved meadows and narrow valleys grow thick covers of grasses and other plants, from spring until fall, providing varieties of food for many creatures. Cold-running streams offer near ideal conditions, or so they did prior to white settlements, for an abundance of fish, mainly trout, and also spawning waters for migrating salmon and steelhead. Great stands of pine, fir, cedar, and spruce have given shelter and refuge for both man and beast, as well as materials for making temporary dwellings during the mild seasons. Above this zone lie massive alpine peaks, ridges, and slopes, snow-covered much of the year. This natural mosaic describes the scenes as they existed long before any human eyes ever beheld them.

Some few hundred years or so after Lassen Peak was created, the first humans found their way onto its surrounding landscapes. They were stone age people whose ancestors presumably had crossed the ice bridge from Asia onto North America. Historical evidence gives no account that human conflict, hunger, or other incentives caused these aboriginal folks to settle in the "Lands of Lassen." Archeological finds and the legends of Indian tradition are our only guides.

Before humans arrived on these scenes, natural conditions and living communities of both flora and fauna had evolved in response only to their immediate environments. Preservation and renewal depended on the conditions of soil, moisture, air and sunlight peculiar to each specific locale. Major physical disturbances in each environment's geological characteristics also had their impacts. "Mother Nature" was then unchallenged, and only structural disruptions generated by natural forces, such as volcanism, glaciers, water flows and earthquakes brought about new relationships. Such physical transformation derived from evolutionary processes, not contrived or imposed from outside nature's primeval setting. With the arrival of human beings an entirely different set of forces began to emerge, though at first very slowly at the hands of the aboriginals.

A number of tribal peoples shared the Lands of Lassen when the first reported penetration by Europeans in the latter 18th century and early 19th century occurred in what is now Northern California. As stone-age humans, the tribes did not possess the implements that could transform in any noticeable way the land forms and life systems which they found existing there. Native inhabitants dwelt there only as "guests," unable to alter the original nature of things. Volcanism was and continues to be the most powerful among the dynamic forces.

These early Americans inhabited a region that was both profoundly and delicately balanced in terms of the cycles of seasons, interdependent living or "biotic" communities, geolgocial realities, and sustaining forces. Inhabiting this region required maintaining a benign, balanced connection to these indigeous factors. The human capacities, as they were shaped and preserved from generation to generation, fashioned no other alternative, behaving simply in accord with nature's perpetual and self-evolved laws.

Native American Beginnings

The original dwellers in Lassen country came up from the Sacramento Valley and its adjacent rolling hills, which their forebearers had occupied at least four thousand years ago. For reasons still obscure, they were forced into the less hospitable foothills and mountain terrains, around the eighth or ninth century A.D. Oral traditions among some valley tribes attribute a certain "hostility" to the mountain peoples, perhaps due to earlier frictions and to the more harsh nature of their living environments. The region was then in a pure state of nature: no external human influences had ever altered so much as a tree, a rock, a stream or a meadow.

According to archeological findings, their ancestors arrived after the Ice Age. Living still in the Stone Age, they were as culturally developed as other tribes at the time. But their culture, their stock of knowledge and living patterns, had not changed substantially for about four thousand years: that is, from about the time that the Patriarch Abraham set out from Ur on his westward journey, around 2000 B.C., until the 19th century. Comparing the cultural changes occurring over this time span in the two areas (Northern California and the Near East), it would appear that the one was static and the other highly mobile. However, what does the statement mean in terms of capacity to survive in a given environment, or in terms of essential values undergirding human existence? Absence of a written history of the original Lassen peoples prevents any further comparison of how successfully their culture perpetuated their society, as against the same process in Near Eastern cultures. Some clues can be found in examining their ways of life prior to the arrival of the Europeans. In exploring this interest without bias, we can gain something for ourselves and posterity. (For sources, see Notes.)

Territoriality

The Lassen peoples inhabited the slopes, meadows, canyons, forests and foothills of the mountain range in all geographical directions from Lassen Peak.

18

While one cannot speak of boundaries in the modern sense, there were clearly identifiable territories which each tribal group acknowledged to be controlled as domain by their neighbors. (Figure 1-1.) Using the concept of "quadrants" with Mount Lassen in the center, we find on the northeast quadrant the Atsugewi people, whom the white pioneers would later call the "Hat Creeks," because their main habitat lay along the creek bearing that name as given by the settlers.

To their south and extending also westward to the Sacramento River, the Maidu occupied the largest expanse of land which constituted the equal of two quadrants. On the western flank of the mountain range in the final quadrant were the Yana which included a small sub-group called the Yahi, who controlled the southern-most part of that territory. Running north-to-south along the entire western and northern limits of the Yana-Yahi, and to some extent of the Atsugewis, the Wintun people occupied the core of the central Valley. It was presumably the Wintun Indians who, having arrived later in California than had the Yana, had forced the smaller Hokan-speaking tribal groups to settle in the higher elevations. For practical purposes, we apply the term "Lassen Peoples" to the Atsugewi, Maidu, and Yana-Yahi tribal groups.

Each group's territory included one or more important streams flowing down from Mount Lassen and other nearby mountain peaks. In the northeast, Hat Creek and the Pit River were the main ones for the Atsugewi. For their southern Maidu neighbors, it was Butte Creek and the Feather River. The Yana controlled Cow Creek, Bear Creek and most of Battle Creek, while their brother Yahi lived along Mill Creek, Deer Creek and portions of upper Battle Creek. (Figure 1-1.) Altogether these four tribal groups numbered about 4-5,000 near the end of the 18th century, a small percentage of an estimated one hundred thirty thousand Native Americans in California at the time of the first Spanish settlements in "Alta" (upper) California (1769). The Maidu people probably made up nearly one-half of that number with the Atsugewi and the Yana-Yahi people numbering about the same, or between one thousand and fifteen hundred each.

While these populations did not organize, as did most Native American peoples east of California, into distinct and well integrated tribes, they recognized chiefs who held authority over several villages and living units. The Atsugewi, however, recognized an overall chieftain with broader influence. (See Figure 1-2, Chief Shavehead.) Their male leader normally possessed unusual abilities and attributes and accumlated more material wealth than did the average male in each communal setting. Chief Shavehead's predecessors were consulted on important problems or issues and would usually decide, in consultation with village headmen, whether to do battle with neighbors over some dispute of grave concern. Beneath the chief, whose eldest son usually succeeeded him, headmen of small villages and clan units held similar authority. Accession to these political roles tended also to come by hereditary succession, but on occasion this rule could be challenged, and even a ruling chief might be deposed if he were generally viewed to be an ineffective leader. Existing archeological finds do not tell us exactly how many villages and dwelling places each tribal group had, but the recollections of the last reported "wild" survivor of the Yahi people, Ishi, provided reasonably good information on such "settlements." Regretfully, many sites were destroyed, overrun, or otherwise desecrated by the European-American intruders and their successors whose economic development projects swept over aboriginal villages and campsites. In most instances Native Americans were killed, or forced to abandon their habitats and enter "reservations" or else simply disperse into white communities.

Territoriality also found expression in language. Three of the tribal groups' tongues descended from the ancient Hokan language family, sometimes also referred to as "Shastanoan" tongues: the Atsugewi, the Yana, and the Yahi. The Maidu people spoke a Penutian dialect, akin to that of the Wintun tribes, who had arrived with a later Indian migration into northern California. This linguistic difference suggests again that the Hokan-speaking peoples had been pushed up into the highlands from the valley country by later arrivals.

Within the Hokan groups, the Yana spoke a dialect somewhat different from that of the Yahi; and both of these differed in some respects from the Hokan of the Atsugewi. Long separation from each other probably accounts for these divergencies. Among the Yahi, there were even some dialectical differences between male and female speakers. This fact reflects a level of cultural refinement or distinction, as well as adherence to prescribed social norms for sexually based relations. Its intent was to control communication along specific paths, in line with a code of social norms. Between tribal entities, communication was very problematic and resistant to cooperation among them, reflecting tribal tenacity to preserve local identity and territory.

Some inter-tribal relationships nonetheless developed through trading and also intermarriage. While the practice was apparently infrequent, brides were on occasion exchanged between tribes. Rare cases of bride-stealing were causes for retribution by the aggrieved party and sometimes led to inter-tribal conflict, or vengeance by one party against the aggressor.

Land Use, Life Styles and Technologies

The term "stone age" culture tells a great deal about human beings' limited physical abilities to shape their environment. While the ancient Nubian-Egyptian and Mayan societies accomplished monumental works without the mechanics of metal implements, their engineering benefitted from a long accumulation of scientific knowledge, a large pool of human labor, and an environment congenial to extensive construction projects. These elements were lacking to the Lassen peoples, whose primary activities revolved around securing their indigenous habitats which provided the bases of livelihood.

The most challenging task facing the aborigines was constructing adequate shelter and other domestic structures, as for storing foods. Although there was some variation among the tribal groups, the most common permanent housing was a conically shaped, A-frame hut made of thick cedar bark placed over wooden poles and branches. They packed soil around the edges to protect against wind and water. In the cook-house, the center of the earthen floor was dug out to an area of perhaps three-to-four feet deep and eight-to-ten feet across, where the hearth was made for heating and cooking. Baskets for food preparation were stored around the perimeter. Typically a small opening at the ground level served for children's entry and exit, while a large hole at the top, reached by climbing notched timbers, provided a door for adults as well as an exit for smoke. Among some villagers this kind of winter house could be fifteen to thirty feet in length, depending on the number of inhabitants. At lower elevations, where food gathering and climate were more congenial, communal dwellings could be much larger and designed for year-round living. Huts for sleeping had similar shapes but somewhat smaller than the cook-house. Depending on family size five to ten persons slept there on mats made of needles and leaves, and under animal pelts of bear, deer, or rabbit skin.

The mountain people made more temporary arrangements during the migratory periods from early summer until fall, because they were more often on the move during the milder seasons. Usually such shelters were made of brush and branches, with some use of bark. Sturdy branches might be propped up against a huge tree or a sharp embankment and then covered on three sides, leaving the front more or less exposed. The Yahi dwellers of the steep Mill and Deer Creek canyons found natural caves as useful refuges, some of which can be observed still today.

Quite primitive indeed were these "homes," as compared to the elaborate uses made by European-Americans of milled timbers, masonry, and metal supports, not to mention glass, tile and concrete. The Lassen builders did not require massive construction for protection against the elements and for preserving food supplies. The Native Americans' demands on the material environment for their shelters were modest, while the Europeans massively exploited nature's elements in order to satisfy their concept of daily comfort and material profit. Lassen country had a plentiful supply of rocks and minerals which could have been utilized by the aborigines for construction purposes. But we can assume that their basic needs for protection, rather than for comforts, were adequately taken care of by more simple dwellings.

Life within the villages and campsites revolved around three requirements: 1) gathering food, all of which came directly from nature, inasmuch as no sedentary agriculture or crop-growing was practiced; 2) the storage and preparation of food; and 3) providing clothing and shelter for families. These activities required the making of basic implements and household wares, left to the men and boys. All tools were made of stone, bone, wood, shells or plant fibers in the tribal area. Occasionally neighboring tribes traded arrowheads for acorns or skins. Chieftains and headmen led hunting and fishing parties in their common territories and also were called upon to organize and manage festive occasions, ceremonies and sweat house sessions. Each tribal village had its "mens' house," a refuge from the congestive domestic activities conducted by the women and girls in the main dwelling. In these separate quarters, fathers bonded with their sons and perpetuated those skills, attitudes and habits becoming an adult male in the community. A small multi-family village, in the declining days of the Yana-Yahi, was described by Ishi. (See Notes.)

Food procurement and meal preparation depended on what nature supplied. To acquire by hand, arrow, spear or net what was available required nothing elaborate. Animal skins had to scraped and dried; bark had to be pealed and sometimes transformed into cords; nuts had to be shelled and ground into meal; various foods must be boiled; dried meats, fruits, insects and fish must be stored away for winter; and so on. Animal intestines served as extra strong cord (similar to "cat gut"), and glue came from boiling fish skins. Basketry could be made so tightly woven as to hold water for long periods of time. To boil liquids a number of stones heated until red hot in the fire were plunged into water, or other liquid, such as a juice, held in baskets. Sometimes animal hides lined the inside of baskets to increase their liquid-holding capacity.

More powerful instruments or tools were made for hunting and fishing. The bow and arrow, the spear, and nets required more skills and ingenuity than were required for domestic arts, except for basketry. In areas where obsidian was plentiful, tribal trading flourished to secure the best arrow heads by those who lacked them, in exchange for staple foods that were in short supply. Fish nets made from fibers and gut ensured a good catch in streams where trout were always plentiful. Each village had its "work house," a place where men made tools, implements and hunting and fishing gear. Flints, cords, hides and other supplies were kept in ornate baskets. (Figure 1-3.) The women worked either outside under cover of trees or in the cook-house, engaging in basket-weaving, clothes-making and food processing.

The methods and schemes, including "tricks," for capturing and killing wild animals were many and varied. In essence, however, they all depended on clever use of the natural surroundings, not on massive use of force. In this approach lay a profound difference between the Native American attitude toward the "kill" and that of the European. For example, deer might be ambushed from several sides of a canyon slope and forced to leap across, and sometimes into, an abyss, causing the crippling or death of one or more animals. On other occasions, brush fires would be started to flush out game. Careful and prolonged stalking of an animal for a day or more aimed at exhausting the animal or causing it to become distraught. Either outcome opened up opportunity for the hunter's arrow or a direct bodily attack. The Native American aborigine applied an ethic related to his taking of animal prey which said that the human aggressor was acting only in terms of survival. Killing was not a wanton or senseless act. The beast was respected and admired for its place in the environment, and in a sense it was praised for this role. This social value governed Indians' relationships with other living things as well.

Various kinds of fish nets, including gill nets, were used depending on the character of the stream, pond or lake. Spearing fish by harpoon was also common. (Figure 1-4.) In most instances, the wit and courage of the fisher and hunter were pitted against the wiles and instincts of animals, fish and birds. There was no such thing as a sudden, powerful blast of a twelve-guage shotgun or a .32 caliber rifle to bring down the prey, whether for pure sport or for food. Lassen natives were appalled at white men who occasionally threw dynamite into streams to "catch" fish.

For the most part, women gathered acorns, seeds, pine nuts, roots, berries and similar plant products. They prepared and cooked foods for their family unit, made baskets and performed most of the domestic chores. Female submission to the male was symbolized by the man's right to marry two or more women, and

23

also to divorce a wife if she did not please him or in some way became unsuited to his tastes. There is no evidence that the wife could reject her mate and also separate. Polygamous families were apparently based on the economic capacity of the male head of the unit to provide and were accepted as a normal life style. Chiefs often had numerous wives and large numbers of offspring. But native parents did not allow themselves to have children indiscriminately. The number of mouths to feed was carefully weighed in sexual conduct and pregnancy. Certain herbs were well known for preventing conception or inducing abortion, and these methods were commonly used. European-American reports of extreme sexual license among California aborigines, beginning at the age of puberty, cannot be arbitrarily applied to Lassen tribes. First, because survival in this rugged region required more control over procreation to limit the number of children. And second, there were reasonably strict rules governing relationships between men and women, as indicated in the Yana-Yahi speech forms and in social habits which regulated intercourse between males and females. The Atsugewi had similar rules.

One criterion of any quality of life is the food base for families and communities. We know that animals, by both instinct and habit, know which foods are nutritious and which are not. Learning from the Native American experience, we find that even in the rather austere and less fertile mountainous areas of California, it was possible to provide an interesting and rich diet. Foods readily available to Lassen natives included all the major proteins, starches and sugars ranging from deer or antelope to eggs and honey and fruits.

While neither a Maidu nor a Yahi housewife would have known the vitamin, calorie or colesterol composition of their foods, long experience and intimate knowledge of the effects of ingestion gave her an excellent "rule of thumb" by which to feed her families. No doubt dependence on the factors of availability, season, and hunters' fortunes were variables over which her culture provided little control, as compared to today's high use of technologies to manage food production and supply. One advantage she had was that natural honey did not have the additive ingredients of today's products.

Social Life, Mores and Beliefs

Aside from the demanding tasks of providing food, shelter, and protection for families, these communal Indian societies found time and need to construct a belief system that explained their universe, to organize festive and recreational gatherings, to devise games and to resolve social problems in orderly ways. The

24

fact that food sources in most of the tribal lands were plentiful, especially game and fish, lessened the time required for building up supplies and afforded time for recreation and other pursuits. Playing games was one of these pastimes.

Guessing games, using either small sticks or stones, was popular. The items might be either shuffled in the hand, or placed in a pile. Participants then had to guess the number, the winner receiving payment in kind. Such games were sometimes played between different villages. A kind of "kick-ball" game involved two sides attempting to scoot a buckskin ball, stuffed with hair, between goal posts at each end of a field, not unlike the game of soccer. It was apparently fair to push, shove or even wrestle an opponent to prevent his or her scoring.

A form of grass hockey, employing sticks for whacking the ball to and fro, was a common sport which included women and children. Children also "played house," in imitation of adults, using dolls and make-shift huts. Villagers also engaged in foot racing, adults sometimes covering many miles, as when the course encircled an entire lake.

On occasion the chief, if he were sufficiently affluent, would organize a feast to highlight inter-village competitions. His contributions were augmented by wild game being hunted and brought in by the men and boys who contributed their prey to the offerings. Festive music, consisting of drums, rattles, whistles, bow strings and singing or chanting usually accompanied the games and other activities. In the chief's sweat-house both men and women danced to the beat of sticks and rattles, usually around a central fire which caused heavy perspiration and, eventually, exhaustion. Whether or not these parties culminated in sexual orgies, as sometimes occurred in other tribal cultures, we have no knowledge. When a dancer had had enough, he or she would plunge into a stream or lake to cool off and then rest. This practice was believed to have healthy effects.

In all these avenues of expression, Lassen's native peoples reflected an ensemble of cultural interests and entertainments that resembled closely those of many other societies. While less sophisticated than some, they nonetheless demonstrated the human yearning for creativity, social bonding, emotional outlets and, of course, procreation. These inclinations extended also to the world of the spirit, in the sense of supra-human powers and influences which reflected a cosmology transcending the earthly human scene. The belief systems of various tribal folk differed in certain respects, but a few essential aspects can be said to represent a general pattern.

The star-lit sky, and especially the moon, gave rise to a variety of imaginations and concepts about life and its origins. In the full moon they saw the figure of a great frog. He was actually moon's wife. The series of moon phases represented the cycle of life, from birth to death. Moon power was acknowledged in various ways, such as holding new-born infants in the moonlight to bring blessings and freedom from illness. Female menstruation was seen to be in cadence with the lunar month. The moon crescent pointed toward good times and fair weather. The deads' departing spirits (souls) went to the heavens and travelled the Milky Way, free from earth's constraints. The stars known as "Seven Sisters" were for some Indians seven maidens who, at a puberty dance, were seduced by Rabbit Boy and were transformed into stars. When sun-moon eclipses occurred, it meant that one or the other had been swallowed by an animal, typically by the wise and clever Coyote.

Several creation myths attributed birth of the human race (usually identified with one's tribal community) to supernatural powers of animals, and notably Coyote. The biological drive and procreative force emerged from these ancestral beings who, simulating humans, sought ways to recreate themselves in a new world. The Atsugewi myth went this way: "The sun and moon were two brothers whom Grey Fox told to climb up into the sky to light the world, the one during the day and the other at night.... Grey Fox first wanted to create two moons and two suns. But Coyote objected saying that it would be too hot. Grey Fox then made only the sun and one moon." (Cited from T. Garth, 1953.) For the Yana, Coyote also instituted death as a permanent condition, with no avenue for resurrection or after-life. The world of work and labor also came at Coyote's command (Maidu myth), because he disagreed with the Creator's plan that life would be fully provided for, as in some paradise, without human work and sacrifice.

Once created in their new earthly setting, people had to find means for maintaining health and curing diseases. This task fell, in the course of time, to the medicine men, or "shamans." Their treatments relied heavily on the psychology of fear and faith, but also included use of herbs, sweating, blood-letting, and fasting. The reliance on mental means is especially interesting, inasmuch as contemporary medical theories attribute significant influence to mind as opposed to material remedies alone. Were the shamans of our aboriginal predecessors so far off the mark in approaching illness from a perspective of psychological treatment? Their incantations, mesmeric rituals, and appeals to the spirit world were perhaps crude forms of metaphysics, but nonetheless metaphysical in character.

A variety of herbs were used for treatment of certain illnesses, such as colds, headaches, rheumatism, snake poisoning, etc. Bathing and sweating were sometimes combined with use of herbs or pine needles. Which root, or seed, or leaf was applied to heal what ailment, was knowledge passed on from generation to generation. There were no medical encyclopedias where treatments were catalogued: It was all in memory! The exact methods for diagnosing and then prescribing treatment were the special domain of these doctors, or shamans. They passed on their wisdom and skills to young apprentices who would one day also enter the healing practice. Just how successful they were, as compared to our practices today, we shall probably never know. It was only with the coming of the white man, who had a very different immune system and pathology, that aboriginal medicine failed its people, succombing quickly to diseases theretofor unknown to them, and therefore without a prescribed remedy or method of treatment in their cultures.

Such were the world and life systems of Lassen country peoples. Their cultures spanned every significant aspect of what the European claimed to be necessary and proper conduct on this earth. The essential differences between the two lay in technologies, in degrees of sophistication and in universality. If religion and theology were to be invoked here to differentiate the two worlds, the reader may want to evaluate the efficacy of his or her beliefs in terms of what the Lassen Indian villager sought to accomplish by having recourse to a variety of remedies. Where are the essential divergencies? And how profound are they?

In one additional respect, it is worthwhile to describe further Lassen tribal attitudes toward sexual relationships. Aside from the masculine dominance in the matter of divorce, there was an elaborate set of rules governing attitudes, relations, and personal security. After bonding (marriage), neither husband nor wife was supposed to speak directly to in-laws of the opposite sex. This rule protected them from possible sources of oppressive influence, advantage, incest and abuse. Among the Yana-Yahi, women were addressed in forms of speech distinct from those used to address men. This practice endowed a female, for example, with a certain deference in relation to masculine behavior. While marriages of young people were usually arranged between parents, involving a "bride price," it was also common for two young people to fall in love. When they agreed to sleep together (even though they may have had previous intercourse), the two were considered bonded if parents did not object. The husband-to-be then owed his father-in-law a "bride price," which he paid either in "money" (beads, shells, etc.) or in goods. So far as real-life instances have been reported, the stability of Lassen native families appears to have exceeded that which we observe in our modern societies.

These first Lassen peoples observed a certain decorum and gentility in social intercourse. It was expressed in both a formal deference toward members of the opposite sex and a caring solicitude for others' well-being. Separate dialects in the Yana-Yahi tongue for male and female speakers illustrates this social-psychological disposition. There is a formality to be followed, but with it goes a protection for the individuality and dignity of the one being addressed. An expectant mother received special care and attention, and after the birth she also enjoyed special considerations and ate foods that would be beneficial to the nursing infant. On the other hand, if a husband had proof of a wife's infidelity, or even of sexual overtones and playful enticements toward a man, he would beat her physically, or perhaps divorce her outright.

Accounts of what may be called the Native American "character," or personality traits, reveal human beings with a solid, positive sense of self-respect and of respect for both other human-beings and the natural world. One of the most telling of such accounts is that given by Professor Alfred Kroeber (University of California), who became a close friend of the Yahi tribal survivor, Ishi. Dr. Kroeber characterized this man as extremely sensitive to and observant of the rights of others, their inherent right to be individual, to have their space undisturbed by others. According to Kroeber, Ishi was every whit a gentleman, a caring person, a proud man, adding that, "He was the most patient man I ever knew." Yet, he was popularly referred to as the wild man from the stone age, a savage without civility or proper manners, whose people were doomed to abandon their way of life because they were "in the way" of the newcomers. As for table manners, Ishi used fork and knife handily but felt they were unnecessary tools for proper nourishment of the body. When asked about his cultural preferences, Ishi replied: "The white man knows many things, and much that is false; but I know nature, which is always true." If he could have returned to his native area to live, he said he would take from the white man's culture two items: matches, and glue!

It was at this point in cultural development of the aborigines that the pale-skinned humans, arriving in Lassen country primarily from the east, confronted these tribal peoples. The confrontations occurred along every line of Native American existence and organization. No aspect of native culture went untouched by the encroacher. It was total and imperious, fully in keeping with notions of "Manifest Destiny" and Christian self-righteousness. One representative of this culture-bound and racist point of view, Ranger Horace Bell, wrote in 1881:

"We will let those rascally redskins know that they have no longer to deal with the Spaniard or the Mexican, but with the invincible race of American backwoodsmen, which has driven the savage from Plymouth Rock to the Rocky Mountains, and has headed him off here on the western shore, ... and will drive him back to meet his kindred fleeing westward, all to be drowned in the Great Salt Lake." (From, "Reminiscences of a Ranger")

So much for the nobility of one "holy" conqueror. Superiority, Ishi would reply, is not a matter of physical power but of one's capacity to be human.

YUROK
KAROK
LUTUAMI
SHASTAN
WIYOT
ATHABASCAN
CHIMARIKO
YANA
YUKI
WINTUN
POMO
MAIDU
WASHO
MIWOK
COSTANOAN
YOKUTS
ESSELEN
SALINAN
CHUMASH
SHOSHONEAN
YUMAN

1.
2.
NORTHERN
(Atsugewi)
CENTRAL
Lassen Volcanic Nat'l Park
3.
SOUTHERN
4.
Y A H I
5.
6.
(Maidu)

Rivers/Creeks:
1. Sacramento R.
2. Pit R.
3. Cow Creek
4. Battle Creek
5. Mill Creek
6. Deer Creek

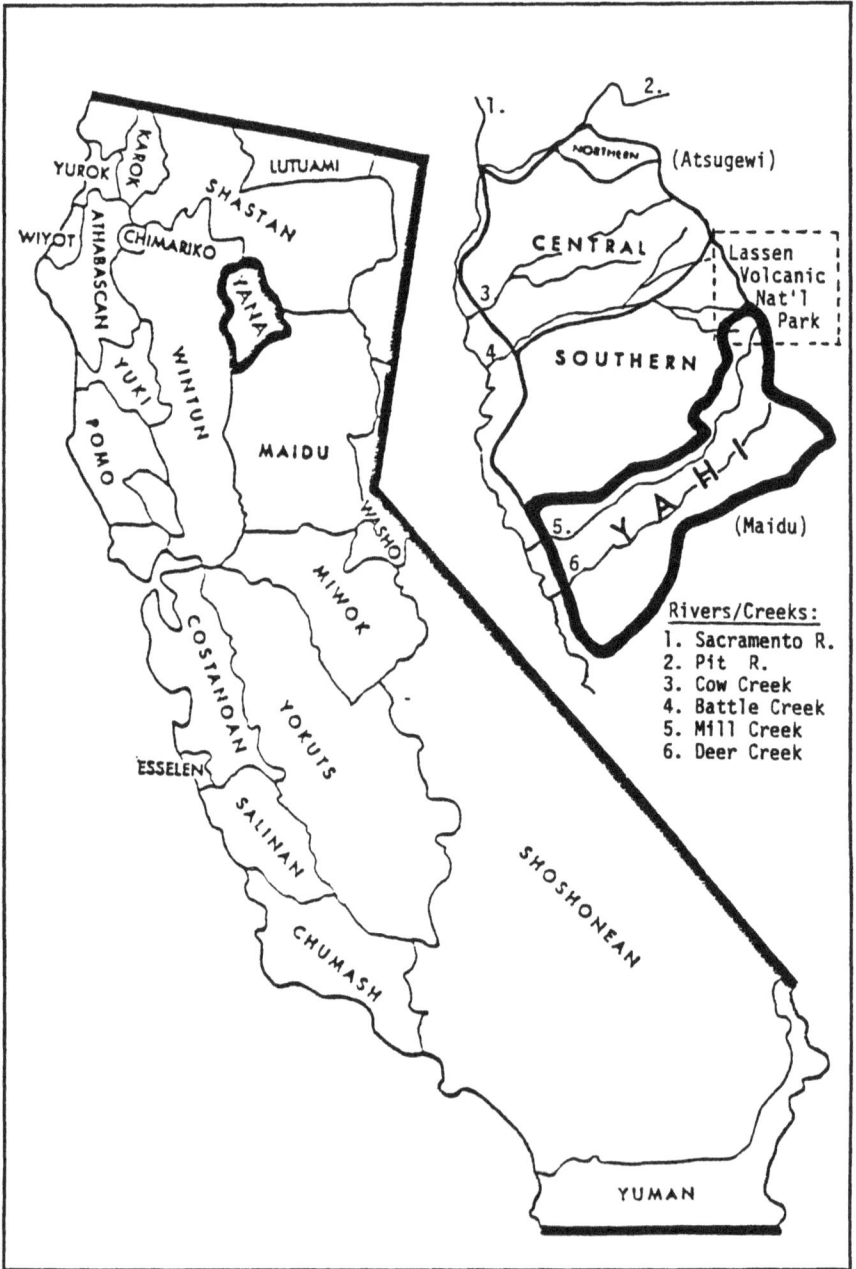

1-1.   Indian California
Inset shows the Yana territory with the Yahi lands in the far south.

1-2.   Chief Shavehead (Atsugewi Tribe)

1-3.   Native American Basketry (Atsugewi)

1-4. Ishi Making a Harpoon

CHAPTER 2

BATTLE FOR THE LANDS OF LASSEN

Preludes to White Supremacy in Northern California
European aggression and domination in "Alta California," as the Spaniards
referred to this region of their North American Empire, date only from the late
1760s with the beginning of the Spanish mission movement: to establish Catho-
lic Church settlements for cultivating the faith among the "heathen." This Spanish expansion stemmed in part from the Spaniards' fear that Russian and British
penetration into northern California would threaten Spain's position to the
south and east.

The Russians, since the explorations of Admiral Bering in the North Pacific
Ocean and Bering Sea in the 17th century, had gradually occupied Alaska and
then explored southward along the Canadian coast, reaching as far as San
Francisco Bay in the 18th century. "Russian Hill" survives today as a name-place
in the heart of the city. About one hundred twenty miles north of the Bay, they
founded a coastal fort, Fort Rossiia (since then renamed simply "Fort Ross"), and
also gave their name to the local river, "Russian River." But the Russians were
interested only in fur trading and garnering food supplies to ship up to Alaska.
They apparently enjoyed a compatible relationship with the coastal Native Americans, with whom they traded. Except in Alaska, they did not attempt to force
Christianity onto the local population. And, they had no contacts with the valley
or mountain tribes east of Fort Rossiia, so far as records indicate. (See Notes for
references.)

The British excursions (long after Sir Francis Drake's visit by ship to San
Francisco Bay in 1579) had been preceded by French trappers-voyageurs, probably
representing the Northwest Company in Montreal, who ventured into Idaho,
Oregon and the upper reaches of California. Well organized British-sponsored
parties, such as those led by Peter Ogden, Michel Laframboise and Alexander
McLeod, traversed parts of north central California, including Lassen country,
during the 1820s to 1840s. An American party under a trapper named Jedediah
Smith ventured into the upper Sacramento Valley in 1828. All these expeditions

made cursory contacts with the aboriginal peoples, sometimes with sore losses of supplies and animals. But there are no recorded bloody battles between the two sides at the time. The fact that the white intruders were primarily after furs, then plentiful, and not the confiscation and settlement of native territories, explains the lack of major hostilities.

The Spanish missionairies and their civilian settlers did not establish their haciendas, churches and other institutions in the Sacramento Valley proper, but reached only about forty miles northeast of San Francisco Bay, at Solano, in Sonoma County, the farthermost mission. (Figure 2-1.) Nor was the Spanish presence large, numbering only between 4,000 and 5,000 around 1820. Although the missionaries occupied Native American lands, forced some of the natives into obligatory labor, and baptized them into the church, their methods did not normally lead to harsh confrontations, widespread brutality, or warlike hostilities. These came after the "mission period," from 1830 on, when some of the non-missionary settlers occasionally used brutal measures. The Vallejo family were notorious for their expeditions against and cruelty toward tribal peoples in the Napa - Sonoma area. The Spaniards and Mexicans had sought primarily to incorporate the natives into their social and economic system, for their own benefit. But there was no policy of arbitrary exclusion or annihilation of Native Americans. With the coming of the Anglo-American settlers, it became by-and-large a different matter.

In an effort to establish Mexican hegemony throughout the Sacramento Valley, the Government of Mexico (after 1821) proceded to issue land grants, termed "rancherias," to willing settlers regardless of their country of origin. The earliest known Spanish penetration of Lassen country came in 1821, when Don Luis Arguello's party sighted Lassen Peak and named the mountain "San Jose." By 1848, when California was forcibly ceded to the United States by Mexico, it had made many land grants along the Sacramento River. Most lay in the midst of Wintun tribal territory but some were adjacent to the Lassen mountain tribes. One grant was to Peter Lassen, a Danish-born prospector, who established his "Rancho Bosquejo" in 1844. In rather small numbers at first, emigrants like Lassen began to ranch and develop economic enterprises, doing some trading with the aborigines but also forcing some of them to work for the newcomers. Among the valley tribes there are a few reports of isolated conflicts but generally the white presence was not at first perceived to be a menace to their survival. The situation soon changed, however, and the future of aboriginal Californians would be seriously threatened. (See Notes for references.)

Emigrant Occupation: Extermination of the Aborigine (1846-1870)

Fundamental to penetration and dominance by white settlers were their communication systems. Lassen and other pioneers developed wagon trails into northern California through the southern Cascades: The Applegate Trail, the Nobles Trail, and the Lassen Trail (See Figure 2-1). After 1846, and particularly following discoveries of gold fields, the human flow along these trails swelled, bringing thousands of settlers and adventurers into the mountains and valleys. By the mid-1850's over 3,000 people and 30,000 head of livestock had crossed the mountains into "Indian territory." A new era had dawned.

In 1854 the U.S. Army commissioned Lieutenant Edward Beckwith to chart a railroad line through Lassen territory. He favored the Nobles Trail route, but later a more southerly passage through the Sierra Nevada Range was chosen. Wagon roads remained the main carriers of people and goods across the Cascades: a road from Red Bluff to Susanville (similar to the present auto highway), and one from Chico to Susanville. Both linked up with the main trails across the Great Basin in southern Idaho and northern Nevada and were the principal access routes. The Pacific Railroad founded the "Tehama County Wagon Road" in 1863, which operated as a toll road as far as the village of Mineral. In 1864 J.C. Tyler bought that section of it. In the northeast area, the Lockhart Road linked Manzanita Lake with Yreka, adjacent to Oregon Territory. Boat traffic could navigate the Sacramento River as far as Red Bluff, which served as a northern port for budding settlements needing supplies shipped from San Francisco and Oakland. By 1870 a rail line ran from Red Bluff and Chico to Oakland, greatly facilitating economic development and trade.

As homesteaders (Lassen, Bidwell, Ide, Payne, Reading and many others) established farming, ranching, and prospecting enterprises, their domains extended more and more out of the valley floor and up into the foothills and canyons surrounding the Lassen region. This expansion first took its toll of wild life and fish whose sources of food and clean water were rapidly reduced. In turn, the native tribes found their game disbursed, decimated, or otherwise so disturbed as to create serious problems for their food supply. Meadows and grasslands became cattle ranges, and domesticated animals competed with both wild animals and Native Americans for the same foods, including acorns, nuts, seeds and plants.

Many settlers like Peter Lassen were also gold prospectors, but the Lassen region was not productive, so other minerals and timber were sought instead.

One of these early miners was Mathias Supan (1817-1904), an Austrian immigrant who in 1853 began mineral prospecting. In 1865 he obtained acreage with sulphur and other mineral deposits near Lassen Peak. Later this enterprise became known as The Supan Sulphur Works.

Another homesteader, Robert Anderson, arrived from the east in 1857 and soon went into the cattle business. His herds grazed on land traditionally used by antelope and deer, in the area of Mill Creek and Deer Creek which flowed into the Sacramento River. He also engaged in farming but was most concerned for the better part of ten years with the "savage Indians" who, he claimed, "infested the region where [he] lived."

White ranchers and entrepreneurs were usually short of labor. Forced conscription and kidnapping of Native American families became standard practice, although apparently some Indians joined the rancherias of their own will. In particular, the Maidu people were more docile on the whole than were other Lassen tribes, many of them willing to become useful in the ranch economy of the newcomers. Even so, they had some battles and skirmishes with settlers. The Yana-Yahi, however, for the most part resisted integration more vigorously and sought ways to stand off against the settlers, much as they had previously defended their territory from neighbors. They had also some times foraged in the valley, causing friction with the Wintun tribes, who referred to them as hostile. Faced with multiple settler threats to their existence, occasional Indian raiding parties struck the white settlements and range lands, stealing livestock, sacks of flour, and other stores they could carry away. Most of these reported attacks came from the Yana-Yahi peoples, but whites had occasional problems with Maidu and Atsugewi resistance also. The Maidu lost around three hundred fifty killed in resisting white aggressors.

Physical conflicts were not the only source of threats against the survival of Native Americans. From the first contacts by Spaniards and other Europeans with them, communicable diseases spread first through the coastal and valley dwellers: small pox, chicken pox, measles and venereal diseases at length took heavy tolls among people whose immune system was so very different from that of the Europeans. In some instances, 75% to 30%, or more, of the native communities were wiped out in just a few years. The epidemic of 1833, possibly from measles, was probably the worst one. This factor alone significantly weakened aboriginal capacity to withstand the European advance. And we know even less about its psychological disturbances and impacts which caused untold stress and depression.

The first reported concern of settlers with "Indian" hostility appeared in a Sacramento newspaper in April, 1850. Thereafter, hostile attitudes by whites toward the Lassen natives began to fester and intensify. Pinpointing the blame for this trend in retrospect is not easy, inasmuch as both sides had grievances.

Emigrants on the trails, as described in the account by J. Goldsborough Bruff, were rarely molested by the aborigines. Peter Lassen reported only one hostile encounter with the Yahi, who had stolen cattle in Mill Creek canyon. Lassen's party attacked their village, after which the Indians made a peace offering. On Lassen's Deer Creek trail which crossed the very heart of their territory, there were no reports of whites being ambushed or molested. Even when the Red Bluff toll road passed through Battle Creek Meadows, a Yana-Yahi camping area, and when cabins and a general store were built at the site in 1865, named Mineral, the tribes whose lands were occupied did not mount raiding parties against these sites. What raids were made on ranches at lower elevations aimed basically to augment their food supply and, on a very few occasions, to avenge the slaughter of their own people.

Aggressive forays for food mounted throughout the 1850s and brought almost instant retaliation by whites in two ways: direct armed attack by bands of whites and forcible removal at gunpoint under the U.S. Army's Pacific Command and Bureau of Indian Affairs to hastily arranged reservations, such as Nome Lackee in the valley and Round Valley in distant Mendocino County. Posses composed of self-appointed vigilantes made excursions into tribal lands of the Yana, Yahi and Maidu. One mass removal of over four hundred and fifty Yana took place in 1863. The Army rounded up families indiscriminantly and, led by a Captain Starr, they marched under guard toward the Mendocino County reservation. En route nearly one-half of them perished or were left behind due to illness. After their arrival, most of the Yana abandoned the site to find their way back to their points of origin. By the mid-1860s the Yana were all but finished and the Maidu cowed into submission. Those who remained were broken in spirit and succumbed easily from poor diets, disease and despair. Some resorted to alcohol, one of the white man's potent "instruments of control."

Only the Yahi continued to be hostile from their almost impenetrable canyon retreats in Mill Creek and Deer Creek. On two occasions they captured and murdered several children and a woman while stealing flour, supplies, heifers and horses. These human atrocities were in principle inexcusable, but they were understandable nonetheless, as a response in-kind to the white policy of mass killings of their people, including women and children.

For any native mountain dweller who dared to resist and even mount reprisals against the foreigner, retribution came swiftly and powerfully. Operating beyond the control of both U.S. military units and the newly formed State Government of California (1851), citizen-led posses of revengeful armed bands combed the hills, canyons and mountain slopes for Indian villages and hiding places. One vigilante organization, called the "Oroville Guards," set their own rules for hunting down the Yana-Yahi in particular. The U.S. Government actually offered bounties for Indian scalps, an incentive which incited even more brutal attacks and relieved the Government from trying to deploy regular Army units, unaccustomed to fighting in the chapparal and canyon country. On two attempts to search out and capture the Yana-Yahi, the Army failed miserably and became the subject of jokes and derision by the settlers. The reliance on armed citizen bands of cutthroats then heightened.

Key local vigilante leaders during this period were Robert Anderson, sheriff of Butte County, his buddy and tracker, Hiram Good, and Sam Moak, a New Yorker whose only vocation was killing Indians. These men got to know the canyon lands well and they headed up most of the posses on the west slopes of the Lassen range. After each foray into the hills, they strung up their scalps outside their ranch homes. Time after time, groups of twenty-five, thirty-five, forty, and even up to fifty men, women, and children were hunted down and brutally murdered by high powered rifles. Sometimes these outlaws employed the Gatling gun, a forerunner of the modern machine gun. One gallant Indian hunter complained to his fellow posse members that his .56 caliber rifle was too powerful, because he said it "tore up" the children too much. So, to ease his conscience and satisfy his human sensitivity, he decided to kill them with only a .38 revolver! Stone age warfare was no match for these instruments of death, nor for the murderous onslaughts of the new invaders. (See Notes for first-hand accounts.)

When tribal attacks struck ranch families, white reprisals sometimes included murdering the innocent. Posse members would search a ranch house where friendly Indians worked. If they happened to be members of the targeted tribe, posse members then dragged them out into the open and killed those defenseless people for no reason at all, except that they were "no good injuns." Women and children received the same treatment as men. This reign of terror eventually cowed Lassen's remaining Native Americans into submission. But the Yana-Yahi people had for the most part to be hunted down and slaughtered like animals.

In other areas of Northern California, U.S. Military units conducted a more orderly and less bloody program of displacing the aborigines. In Modoc country northeast of Lassen, however, the Army fought a long, fierce battle against Chief Kintpuash ("Captain Jack"), who was eventually hung in 1893 for his native heroism.

The sad instances of brutal vigilante pursuits occurred mostly during the period 1855-1875, twenty years during which, along with disease, hunger and related causes of death, over 4,000 Lassen Indians were practically exterminated by the white settlers and vigilante "law enforcers." Although a few remnants continued either to live as best they could alongside the newcomers and with other tribal groups, or to retreat into years of hiding and obscurity, the 4,000 years of native "peace with nature" came to a resounding, violent end. Henceforth, the Lands of Lassen became the province of new American entrepreneurs and adventuresome pioneers. While Peter Lassen and his friends, such as J. Goldsborough Bruff and John Bidwell, might be termed well meaning persons, their social values and economic pursuits conflicted so completely with Native American culture, that space for compromise was practically unthinkable. And indeed the white man had no thought of compromise in his "wonderful new land of opportunity."

Lassen himself, the trail blazer, rancher, mill builder, and prospector was known as a generous individual, but also as inept at managing his resources. His renown in Lassen country was such that both the native names for the mountain (there were at least two) and the Spanish one, Mount Saint Joseph (San Jose), were supplanted by white settlers' common reference to "Lassen's mountain," or just Mount Lassen. Peter Lassen moved to the east slope, near Susanville, in the mid-1850s, where he met his death in 1859, at the hands either of hostile natives or of feuding companions when prospecting for gold. Whether the attachment of his name to the beautiful Fire Mountain and its alpine environment was a plus for posterity can be disputed.

The Last of the Yana-Yahi: An Epitaph

There remains one significant episode in the annals of Lassen natives' confrontation by settlers that speaks more loudly and eloquently than all other accounts. That is the amazing survival of a small band, perhaps only a family or two, of the Yahi people, and their leader, Ishi (translated as "man" in the Yahi-Hokan tongue), referred to earlier. After 1870 only a few isolated sightings were reported by whites of Yahi camps and hiding places. By 1900 it was believed that no members of the tribe had survived. But in 1908 a surveying party stumbled upon a small village in the Deer Creek gorge. Sighting no humans, they ransacked the huts and stores, taking trophies and whatever they could carry off. The Indian settlement was totally demolished. No one knew where the inhabitants went, or how many they were.

Ishi was a child in 1870 when, after the Kingsley Cave massacre above Mill Creek, a few surviving families went into permanent hiding. Retreating to two well secluded areas near the confluence of Deer Creek and Sulphur Creek, they established two small villages. One of them was named Wowunupo mu tetna, or Grizzly Bear's Hiding Place, because in earlier years bears had used a den there. Situated about 500 feet above the Creek on a ledge, it was invisible from any external viewpoint. Tall trees overhung the ledge, providing additional shelter. From the ledge down to the Creek the cliff dropped straight down, so no direct access from the creek bank was possible. To enter and exit the village, the Yahi families crawled on all fours through thick growth of scrub oak and other brush along an almost indistinguishable trail. The largest dwelling was a two-room, conically shaped hut for sleeping and eating. A smokehouse, store room, small pool or reservoir of water, and toilet area completed the village amenities. Simple but adequate for all essential needs. The other village had about the same features. The surveyor team had destroyed one of these two villages in 1908. In these settings, the few remaining Yahi people had lived for approximately forty years before their numbers were reduced to a lone individual.

In August, 1911, an emaciated, weary human being emerged from this den of obscurity and gave himself up to the Sheriff of Butte County, at Oroville about thirty miles due south of Deer Creek Canyon, in Yahi territory. Apparently hunger and immense loneliness brought him to abandon his beloved homeland. His bitter, isolated and long endurance testifies both to his determination to survive as a member of the Yahi Tribe and to the cultural values undergirding such a commitment.

After his physical and moral rehabilitation, Ishi became the confidant of anthropologist Dr. Alfred Kroeber at The University of California in Berkeley and a primary source for recording Yana-Yahi history, ethnology, language, and habitats. After five years (1911-1916) of close relationship with him, Kroeber acknowledged that this man was a gentle, considerate, noble, and intelligent human being, one who had mastered the "philosophy of patience." His "stone age" culture and upbringing were in no way a detriment to his ability to behave in civil and compassionate ways. But his people had been hunted and slaughtered by whites whom he knew not. Now, he befriended them and was also at last befriended. Ishi had had no choice but to join the powerful invaders, or else die alone. Choosing to immerse himself in white society testifies to his courage and also to his will to leave for posterity something from his people's heritage. We are the richer for his choice. (See Notes for the primary sources on Ishi.)

Upon Ishi's death in March, 1916, there were no known representatives of the Yana-Yahi people to carry on the heritage. Residents of Native American descent in the Lassen area tell us that not all surviving members of these and other tribal groups were willing to identify themselves, out of fear of reprisal and in respect for their ancestors. A number of Hat Creek Indians continued to live in Atsugewi areas into the twentieth century. A few of their traditional cultural ways have been preserved, such as basket weaving.

Some elders still retain knowledge about natural foods (roots, plants, berries, etc.) consumed for centuries by their forbearers. A few Maidu tribal descendants also continued to live within sight of Fire Mountain. But our knowledge of the Lassen peoples today depends primarily on archeological findings, which have yet to be fully explored, provided economic development within the Park does not destroy the known sites and others yet to be discovered.

Settler Designs on the Lands of Lassen (1875-1915)

In addition to the ranching, lumbering and mining pursuits by white settlers, they and governmental (federal and state) authorities sought to explore and then exploit the region's other natural resources. Geological and scientific inquiries began at first from curiosity and conjecture. The Native Americans knew about volcanism and referred to "Brokeoff Mountain" much as would the Europeans, calling the Lassen range "the long high mountain that was broken." A prospector, G.K. Godfrey, climbed Lassen Peak in 1851 (though he claimed Peter Lassen had already done so). Miners' expeditions were carried out in 1850, 1862 and 1864, with little success. In 1863 the California State Geological Survey under William H. Brewer explored the mountain and scaled its summit. Geologist Dr. Harvey W. Harkness conducted a more focused investigation in 1874, and in 1878 Lieutenant Samuel E. Till made an extensive survey which extended as far as Susanville. The first complete geological atlas of the area was published in 1895, based on Joseph S. Diller's reconnaissance of the whole of Northern California (1883-85), which emphasized Lassen volcanism. Modern geology of Lassen is based on the later thorough work of Professor Howell Williams of The University of California, who during 1926-32 produced a full documentation of the Massif's characteristics.

These many expeditions and explorations went hand-in-hand with efforts by various economic interests to extract wealth from the mountain region and to establish commerce there. Small summer resorts grew up on the southern and northern slopes of Mount Lassen by the 1870s. A hotel keeper by the name of Benjamin Loomis established his family home near Manzanita Lake (Atsugewi land). In the 1880s a prospector named Edward Drake homesteaded in Warner Valley (Maidu territory), also known as "Hot Springs," where he acquired extensive acreage. The Klotz family homesteaded in McCumber Flat in 1885. (Figure 2-2.) All these early efforts were forerunners of later "tourist businesses" and small enterprises, including cattle ranches within the future domain of the national park.

More ambitious enterprises came with the Northern California Power Company, the Shasta Electric Power Company and eventually the Pacific Gas and Electric Company (PG & E), which sought means to generate power from Lassen's water resources. Streams were harnessed by flumes for water power and to float cut lumber to lower elevations to be transported to urban areas. Streams were dammed to feed the flumes. Shake-making prospered for a while. Most of these efforts were short-lived, however. Logging and livestock remained the most successful profitable pursuits, competing with each other for land use and causing extensive damage to the environment. Cattle and sheep over-grazed grasses, herbs, and shrubs on slopes and riparian areas, activating soil erosion and stream pollution. Loggers' massive removal of trees adjacent to meadows and streams also produced erosion and pollution. Spawning waters for fish were seriously jeopardized, and natural feeding grounds for wild ungulates were molested and sometimes obliterated. But the shear abundance of natural resources, hitherto untouched by humans, blinded exploiters' eyes to their rapacious attitudes and the tolls they exacted from Mother Nature.

One historical account of the relationships which gradually developed between the new white settlers and the original, native inhabitants reflects the general attitude which the newcomers had toward those whom they had completely dispossessed. A few Maidu families acquired ranches themselves, in imitation of the white settlers. But they also engaged in part-time work for the whites. These folks, as the tale goes, came down "into Sierra Valley in the 1880s and 1890s during the hay and grain harvest time and were welcomed, as they were good workers." The story-teller did not consider whether the Maidu had any choice in the matter, or whether or not they would have preferred to recover their traditional lands. It was just assumed by white settlers that the new relationships were

43

the right ones for all concerned. For them, there was no culture clash or cultural choice. Use of the land, water and air was a one-way street controlled by the new landlords, white settlers.

Without any guiding policies, controls or monitoring, economic development efforts began by the turn of the century to take heavy tolls on the once pristine alpine region. Under the growing influence of conservationists led by Clifford Pinchot in the U.S. Department of Agriculture, the local U.S. Forest Service began to consider means to halt the degradation of forest lands by over-grazing, reckless logging, power-generating projects, and excessive hunting and fishing practices.

The battle lines were no longer those drawn between the Native American inhabitants, with their benign impacts on nature, and the European-American settlers with their resource-hungry projects. The new array of forces had the preservationists, following the influence of naturalist John Muir, in opposition to those who envisioned natural preserves as hosts to "many users," a philosophy championed by Forest Bureau Chief Pinchot, a neo-conservationist. Both movements, however, saw the need for federal and state management of the nation's remaining natural resources, such as the Lands of Lassen, crowned by Fire Mountain, represented. (See Notes for studies on this period.)

There was, in a sense, a third constituency involved in this struggle. It was made up of local people and their political representatives who saw the beauties and resources of the Lassen region as values in and of themselves to be protected and preserved for future generations. Some leaned in their attitudes toward Muir, while others opted for a more utilitarian concept. But all were united in the purpose to design some plan for stopping the steady erosion of the region's natural features and for nationalizing extensive areas of alpine domain. At this stage of development, preservationists did not include Lassen's Native American cultures as part of the concept. Those cultures already lay in dusty oblivion and in a state of almost complete destruction, with no one to speak for them, except Ishi and his university entourage.

Prominent leaders of the conservation efforts included U.S. Congressman John E. Raker (originally from Illinois), and U.S. Forest Supervisor Louis A. Barrett. The Forest Service proposed in 1902 setting aside 750,000 acres as the "Lassen Peak Forest Preserve," and by 1905 Barrett's domain included three million acres of forest under Federal protection. But his staff of two or three persons was unable to exercise much control. He and local citizens petitioned President Teddy Roosevelt in 1906 to declare parts of Lassen country national

44

preserves outside the national forests. Barrett followed up this action with detailed reports on the geological and scenic values of the area, as well as on threats to the natural endowments. The Departments of Agriculture and Interior concurred, and in May, 1907, the President declared that two national monuments, totalling just 6,400 acres (Lassen Peak and Cinder Cone), be created. This act laid the foundation for later development of a genuine national preserve englobing most of the area surrounding Lassen Peak.

Congressman Raker, his family and friends, and many local citizens rallied around the idea of creating such a national park. After several unsuccessful attempts to have his House bill reported out of committee during 1912-14, Raker was helped by a mighty force, Fire Mountain itself. In May, 1914 forest rangers sighted billowing ash clouds rising hundreds of feet into the air: Fire Mountain had begun to erupt! Within hours the rare event was communicated across the nation and abroad. Mount Lassen had suddenly attained a notoriety and interest that assured it a place in history and among the nation's foremost monuments. The violent eruptions the following year, in May, 1915, aroused even more worldwide interest. (Figures 2-3, 2-4.)

Armed with this advantage, Raker finally gained top political support in Washington for his national park proposal. On August 9, 1916, President Woodrow Wilson signed the bill establishing Lassen Volcanic National Park. Raker, who died that same year, had garnered strong support both in Washington and in Northern California for the final effort. Within the supporting groups, there were factions which differed in their views of how the new Park's 79,561 acres should be classified, managed and preserved. While the enabling Act specified that the natural domain should remain "unimpaired" for posterity, it also provided for human "enjoyment" and recreation. These human use provisions were not spelled out or defined. It was possible (according to some) to enjoy a park simply in beholding its beauties and in contemplation; while others saw these words as advocating a variety of recreational pursuits. The act also protected the property rights of a number of landowners within the Park's boundaries, many of whom earned their living there. Several thousand head of livestock, resort facilities, and mineral explorations were among these pursuits. (See Notes for history of this period.)

Mount Lassen's sudden outburst, which devastated thousands of acres of surrounding forests, marked the dividing line between human efforts to promote economic interests at the expense of the natural and cultural heritage of Lassen Lands, on the one hand, and counter efforts to preserve the region in its primitive setting. In an historical sense, it is ironic that the mountain itself had to "rise up" in defence of itself! While it had advocates for its cause, the outcome of the political struggle over its fate was by no means predictable before 1914-15. After 1916, when both Lassen Park and the U.S. National Park Service began a new chapter in American wilderness preservation, the two opposing views about human use of the natural world assumed new postures. But their respective roots were anchored in somewhat the same soil as before. The character of the struggle simply branched out into new forms and shades of meaning.

The next episode in this story traces the origins, in the new Lassen Volcanic National Park, of the controversies, their supporting networks and the precipitating issues. Our story will tell how administration of a national park relates to these questions and, ultimately, its affect on a much larger landscape: The grand mission of the natural and cultural preservation movement in this country. As for the cultural heritage and human survival of remaining Native Americans in the area (whose population had, before 1850, counted about 5,000), the vital questions became, Who was there left to speak for them? What remained of their heritage?

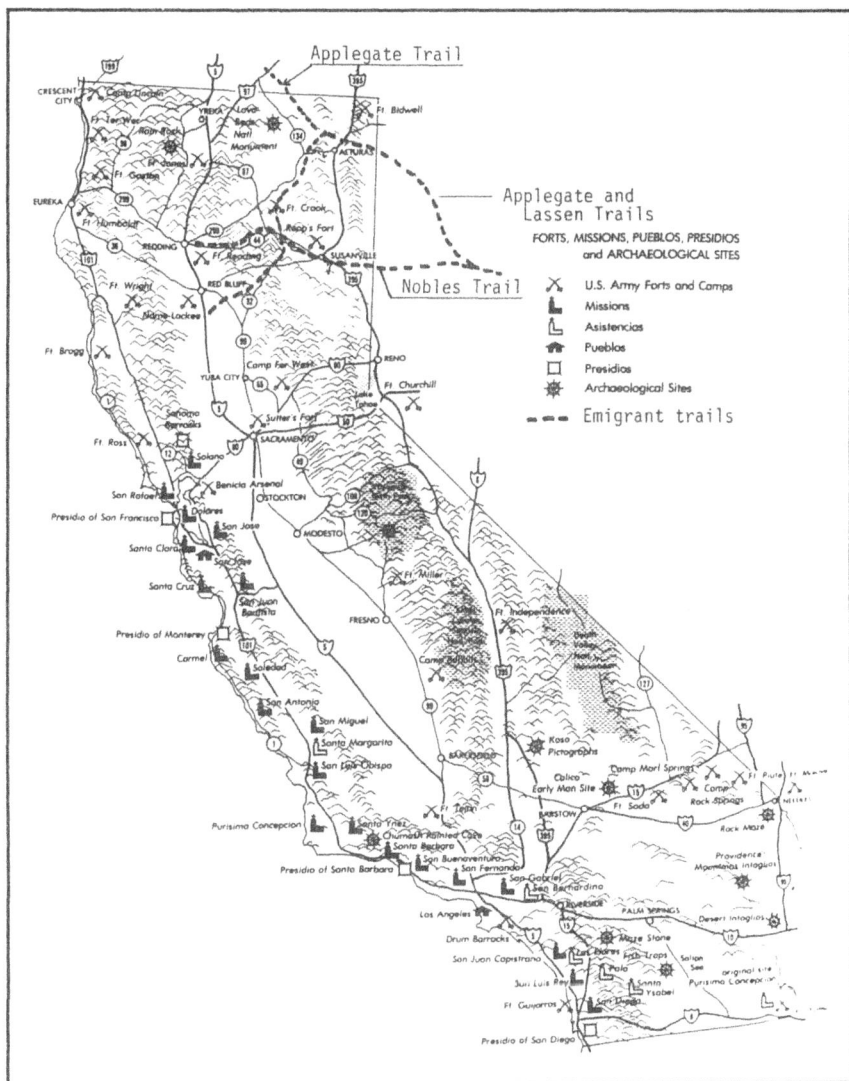

2-1. European-American Settlements and Missions, ca. 1850.

2-2. Early Settlers in Lassen Country (Klotz Ranch, 1885).

2-3. First Eruption of Lassen Peak (May, 1914).

2-4. Devasted Area in Lassen Park (1914-15 eruptions).

CHAPTER 3

RETURN TO WILDERNESS: SEARCHING FOR FOUNDATIONS
(1916 - 1956)

Backgrounds to the Problem

Fire Mountain's eruptions were like a declaration of war against those white settlers who had for over a half-century marred its beauty, pillaged its resources and desecrated native cultures for personal, selfish and wanton advantages. The volcanic outbursts also warned those working and living in its vicinity about the unpredictability of natural disasters. In effect they brought a halt to unbridled exploitations of Lassen's endowments. While some settlers pursued interests that were useful and environmentally benign, many others had no regard whatsoever for conserving, renewing or protecting the region's natural attributes and cultural legacies. The latter included extractive, timber and energy companies intent on a quick return. The worst among these human predators had been ravaging Lassen country's natural resources for decades. Fish and wild mammals rapidly diminished in number and variety. Gone forever were the innocent and reverent aboriginal ideal of balance and harmony between the human and the natural, and the social value which saw the human being as a part of, not superior to, the natural world.

Imbedded in these divergent relationships were a number of deep-rooted differences over the proper human approach to protecting the Lands of Lassen. These differences persisted after the U.S. Government declared the region a natural sanctuary. By creating the National Park Service (NPS) in 1916, Federal policy aimed to set a new course for safeguarding America's natural and cultural endowments, including historical heritages, from threats of misuse and degradation. Private philanthropic interests also joined in this ambitious effort. Notwithstanding this new trend, competing social forces sought to influence if not control the preservation movement, giving rise to major conflicts over managing parks and monuments. Park management confronted these contending influences in almost every aspect of protection and preservation.

Implicit in the establishment of such a wilderness area as Lassen was the need for the general population to relearn the values and realities of nature in its primitive state. These elements had been practically lost during a century or more of industrial and urban encroachments. Both protection and education required a system of management capable of responding to each task and to the tensions created by competing segments of the public striving to control ways in which that dual mission would be carried out. Parallel to the educational concern ran a strong current of recreational interests, including hunting and fishing, supported by ardent advocates who championed the "freedom of the West" ethic, untrammelled by any appeals of social conscience, idealism and nature worship. Initially park managers had practically no guidelines to go by and faced formidable challenges of building new kinds of organization.

At the outset, new patterns of control and management emerged at the Federal level seeking to gain footholds within the new agency itself. NPS was a new kid on the block. Its neophyte leaders could not overnight write their own agendas, free of influences stemming from older units in both the Interior and Agriculture Departments. These departments had previously governed the territories now included within NPS jurisdiction. Then there was a series of specific areas of conflict that arose and still continue today to plague park managers and users.

To set the stage for these discussions, our story begins with the development and management of Lassen Park during its first forty years. It took that long to define enduring policies, create a framework for governance and forge a firm and stable management system accountable to government and the public. Along side these painstaking tasks there was the need to create a public awareness that a national park such as Lassen could not preserve its indigenous character while succombing to and serving all the diverse human interests intent on enjoying its resources. Without such awareness, the very concept of park itself would fail to have meaning, and public ignorance or carelessness could lead to permanent defacement and impairment. Without that awareness, political whims imposed on park managers by pressure groups or career office-holders might breed a climate of opportunism, neglect or abuse and eventual degradation.

It may seem irrelevant at this point to recall that the original native dwellers knew, by natural instincts, that human impacts had to be restrained, if not measured, if both nature and man were to survive. But this meant that they did exercise a kind of management of their domain, which should have received careful consideration by the new federal custodians as they conducted their decision-making work. Little did they realize how much traditional wisdom they were ignoring. (See Notes for sources.)

Fundamental to Lassen Park's creation was the philosophical as well as legal principle which served as cornerstone to all national parks: a national park preserve would not be subject to economic development for commercial gain. Legislation submitted to Congress before 1916 by Representative Raker and Senator Reed embraced this concept. A national conference held in March, 1915, on the Berkeley campus of The University of California under Stephen Mather's leadership also supported this basic premise. Politically, Mather and Albright were Teddy Roosevelt Progressives who championed both conservation of resources for the nation's future, and preservation of certain natural domains for their intrinsic values. In the 1916 election year they leaned toward Woodrow Wilson, not because of common political philosophy but rather for practical reasons linked to Wilson's strong vocal support for the national park concept. An early link was also established with Herbert Hoover who, as Federal Food Administrator during World War I, ordered that sheep be removed from Yosemite National Park, notwithstanding the national food emergency.

Prior to 1916, the only measurable development by the Federal Government in the future Lassen Park was the construction in 1908 and in 1914 of fire station lookouts, first at the summit of Turner Mountain and a second on Prospect Peak. Under the direction of the Lassen Forest Supervisor, forest rangers manned these lone lookouts to try to protect the forest from destructive fires. This service responded to both private lumbering interests and the public concern for conservation. But soon after the Park's creation in 1916, the purpose of protection began to change radically, at least in principle. (Figure 3-1.)

In 1918, the U.S. Department of Interior, under Franklin K. Lane, a Californian as were both Albright and Mather, issued an historic policy statement, based on the 1916 Act creating the National Park Service: "The National Parks must be maintained in absolutely unimpaired form for the use of future generations as well as those of our own time; ... they are set apart for the use, observation, health, and pleasure of the people; and ... the national interest must dictate all decisions affecting public or private enterprise in the parks."

This fundamental declaration was to serve as a rough measuring rod for all future development and intervention in the parks. Later, as NPS Director after 1928, Horace Albright reiterated in even more forceful and eloquent terms this unambiguous policy position. He told park employees that he and they must place "our protective arms around the vast lands which may well need us as man and his industrial world expand and encroach on the last bastions of wilderness ." "We must never forget that all the elements of nature, the rivers, forests, animals and all things [that] co-exist with them must survive as well." The natural conditions of America's grand wilderness areas are sacred, and he cautioned, "once opened, they can never be wholly restored to primeval charm and grandeur." Park uses should be geared to the "quality of ... patronage, not by the quantity ... , so that centuries from now people of our world, and perhaps of other worlds, may see and understand what is unique to our earth, never changing, eternal."

Horace Albright's ideals were prescriptions, if not laws, for guiding the work of NPS personnel in an expanding, complex natural domain. By closely adhering to his eloquent appeals, a park preserve such as Lassen could well have approximated the conditions once known to Ishi and his little tribe. The subsequent story about the fortunes of NPS managers, and those who contended for control over the Park's resources, will tell something about the outcomes of Albright's genuine, but perhaps overly optimistic pronouncements during the early days of the National Park Service.

The Collins Era (1922 - 1935)

The enabling Act of 1916 calling for the nationalization of the Lands of Lassen embraced the principle that the new Park should be managed so as to maintain its indigenous resources unimpaired, while allowing visitors a choice of recreation and enjoyment compatible with unimpairment. However, for almost ten years (1916 - 1925), U.S. lawmakers and the Interior and Agriculture Departments practically ignored the new national park by failing to provide National Park Service budgets adequate to its dual mission. Until 1922, it was actually administered by the Forest Service with minimal financial allowances covering only two forest rangers assigned primarily to forest-fire protection work. These men applied the multiple-use concept to their duties, which was the guiding rule for all Agriculture Department land management. They thereby reinforced many of the predatory habits of the settler mentality. But this style of management would soon be challenged.

In that year, NPS appointed its first manager, a single ranger with no staff and a monthly salary of $150, which did not even cover the costs of his only mode of transportation, his horse! Ranger Lynne Walker Collins (he went by Walker Collins) grew up in the farming community of Corning, about fifty miles southwest of the Park and near the confluence of Mill Creek with the Sacramento River. A high school graduate with extensive experience in Lassen National Forest and well known in northern Sacramento Valley towns, he obtained the position in competition with others also seeking this new and challenging job. In August, 1922, using as headquarters an office in the Red Bluff Post Office, forty-five miles distant, he rode his horse up into the mountains to survey his official "fief" and began planning for boundary demarcation, fire lookouts and patrol trails. Forest Service assistance continued on an annual basis and Collins cooperated with a Federal "Engineering and Landscape" unit in San Francisco to plan infrastructure work.

Without secretarial help, Collins recorded things by hand, and so meagre were his financial resources that he sometimes purchased items out of pocket. His first official "Annual Report" to NPS in Washington was a handwritten document in 1925. By this date thousands of visitors were already entering the Park each year. They as well as other users, such as ranchers, lumbermen, and hunters were expected to abide by NPS "Rules and Regulations" issued in Washington and administered by Collins and two seasonal rangers who distributed 10,000 copies to the public. His two seasonal aides were Forest Service employees who knew little about the requirements or objectives of NPS.

Commercial stages as well as private automobiles carried passengers to several points adjacent to and inside the Park. One such route ran from Chester in the southeast to Drakesbad Resort in Warner Valley. Collins had to collect entry fees, camping fees, transport license fees and grazing fees from cattle and sheep ranchers still using park lands. In an attempt to control and regulate the numbers of domesticated hoof animals grazing the meadows and canyons in competition with wild animals, he issued a formal permit stipulating the fees and range for ranchers' animals. Violations of these contracts were frequent, but Ranger Collins and his two assistants could not physically monitor the entire boundary areas of the roadless Park.

During 1925-26 a "Loop Road" project, from the southwest corner around the Peak's base and over to the northwest corner (Manzanita Lake), was begun to improve access by visitors to the heart of the Park and its volcanic features. By the time Walker Collins was appointed Acting Superintendent in 1927, he had created a significant number of management responsibilities for his staff of three officers (including himself):

Boundary and patrol	Visitor services
Road and trail building	Science and education
Fish and wildlife protection	Law enforcement
Equipment and maintenance	Fire prevention and control
Headquarters and outposts	

These managerial functions had more or less simply evolved from the nature of the tasks to be performed. They were influenced too by official interactions between Collins' office in Mineral, where the Forest Service ceded land and buildings to NPS, and NPS offices in San Francisco and Washington. There had been no official organizational chart for Collins to follow. He organized his duties in line with necessary operations and official orders, and with the communications patterns necessary to conduct them. One of his most interesting and fundamental duties was initiating scientific work: geological surveys and study of volcanism, both of which would contribute to the Park's educational mission. While NPS assigned technical and scientific personnel for these projects, it did not appoint a clerk until 1928, nor year-round rangers until 1929! Meantime, visitors arrived in increasing numbers, and the rangers could accommodate 9,000 campers in one season. There is no evidence at all that these folks knew or learned anything about Native American history and culture in this territory, which had ended tragically and brutally some fifty years before. And there was not yet a park naturalist to design educational programs covering such historical and cultural themes.

In the area of protection and wildlife preservation, Collins' small staff could not monitor animal populations on a systematic basis nor prevent illicit hunting and fishing. Partly due to the latter activities, and partly due to increasing numbers of park visitors, wildlife experienced steady declines. Based on limited census taking, certain species diminished rapidly. Black bears numbered only eighteen in 1930, and fifteen in 1935. The mountain lions were down to three by 1935 and the wildcat to twenty-five. While the red fox dropped from forty to thirty between 1930 and 1935, the coyote was down by two-thirds, from one hundred fifty to fifty. The badger suffered the worst: three hundred animals in 1930 down to only thirty by 1935. Only two mammals experienced an increase: the striped skunk (thirty to fifty), and the mule tail deer (from three hundred to eight hundred fifty). With the rapid decline of most species, park staff spent less and less time trying to take count as the years rolled by. "Return to wilderness" had little meaning for most animals inside the Park and sound management plans were not to be developed and financed until well after World War II. The limited evidence that park staff had indicated that native life forms were out of phase with their original ecological relationships and that human impacts and predation had taken heavy tolls among most species, and were probably still taking their toll even under park management.

Management capabilities could barely match visitor demands, and in this stark reality lay one of several major contradictions between the essential purpose and mission of the Park, and the human pressures for more and more services and activities: how can park management respond to the requirements of restoring and maintaining the preserve in a natural state of unimpairment while lacking the resources to control the social pressures coming from the many different categories of park users? It was human community versus Mother Nature and her Fire Mountain. This question is related to a second: what effects did this problem have on both the staffing of park personnel and the performance of their duties? Local communities, including their commercial enterprises, State and Federal politicians, and NPS offices at regional and national level all became embroiled in the implications of these questions as Lassen Volcanic National Park took shape and direction during the 'twenties and 'thirties.

Major Administrative and Organizational Tasks

By 1930 the park geologist, Dr. Howell M. Williams (geology professor from University of California-Berkeley) had produced his first major opus on Fire Mountain's geological and volcanic features. It was a kind of blueprint for educating the public about volcanic phenomena of the earth, and also for guiding future development of park resources. The next year the "Loop Road" (officially, the Lassen Park Road), which wound through the heart of the Park was completed, allowing for extensive access to wilderness trails and camping sites. Future penetration of the entire Park, which in 1929 reached a total of 106,372 acres, was thus assured. In 1930 over 32,000 persons and 10,000 vehicles crossed its boundaries. Each year more visitors poured into the wilderness, sprawling out into the woods and meadows once frequented by the Yana, Yahi, Maidu, and Atsugewi peoples, who had altogether numbered around 5,000. Now six or seven times that number each year traversed their once primeval territories.

Superintendent Collins appointed his first Park Naturalist, Russell Farmer, to begin conducting nature interpretation programs for visitors during the summer months. Farmer had use of the new park museum, established with funds, collections, and a building donated by longtime benefactors, Benjamin Loomis and his wife. It was named the Mae Loomis Memorial Museum, in memory of their only daughter. Henceforth archeological specimens, artifacts, and other collectibles could be stored in a safe haven for educational purposes. "Safe" became a relative term, inasmuch as the building was constructed of porous lava rock which easily absorbed moisture from air and soil.

Collins' staff grew painfully slow. In 1931 he had only four permanent employees, and even the park naturalist position was classified as temporary. During the summer season, however, there were over eighty employees tending park operations in various capacities, including road and trail maintenance. Some of these positions were funded by other agencies (Forest Service, Bureau of Roads, Bureau of Land Management, etc.).

Collins himself, having an intimate knowledge of valley communities, did the lion's share of outreach work. He established a "travelling ranger" program and a "School of Lassen" which disseminated information about the Park, its purposes, its resources and its needs to the broad public. He required that his employees, and especially the park naturalists, perform quality work and be fully responsible to both visitors and officials. In 1932 he appointed the first permanent Park Naturalist, Norman W. Scherer, who held a Master of Science Degree from The University of Michigan. So, sixteen years after its establishment, Lassen Park finally got its first full-time, professionally qualified, interpreter-educator. This long delay points up a basic contradiction in NPS and Federal Government policy: The gap between intent and purpose, on the one had, and empirical reality on the other. Hopes and ideals, versus politics and its interplay of influence bargaining. In the joustings between NPS and Congress, Lassen Park carried little weight.

With 60,000 annual visitors by 1932, the demands for basic services and programs, including scientific projects more than doubled in a three-year period: Hikers, campers, backcountry bugs, anglers, amateur and professional scientists (including foreign specialists), and just plain beauty-seekers all wanted services. This human traffic meant more museum displays and guides, campfire talks, interpretive trails, car caravans and inquiry services. Scherer worked diligently for two years, submitting detailed reports to NPS and gaining Collins' unbounded praise. He counted on the Park Naturalist to lay the scientific foundation for both education and planning the Park's development. For reasons not reported to Collins, some bureaucrats in NPS-Washington sought to find fault with Scherer's work, and in 1933 this outstanding naturalist transferred out of the Park. Without consultation with Collins NPS then abolished the position, leaving it vacant for almost two years. Collins was at a loss to understand why. He replied to Washington's criticisms time and again, without getting satisfaction. Future events would confirm that his concern was not without foundation.

Lassen's attributes, especially its alpine and wilderness features, were extremely popular with some visitors. Collins had emphasized these attractions in his reports, highlighting his conviction that rugged outdoor experiences and the great natural beauties of the Park were its most valuable assets, inspiring in people "a further appreciation, a greater attitude of inquiry toward nature at large." This rustic, unsophisticated orientation was in keeping with Collins' own background and character, nurtured as he was in a rural environment. There was no taint in his approach of the "amusement park" mentality, which had already stained the awesome beauties of Yosemite National Park.

Among Lassen's admirers were then President Herbert Hoover, also a Californian, and his associates. They made occasional fishing trips to the cold mountain trout streams. Superintendent Collins and his rangers naturally accommodated such guests within the purview of their assignments. Other politically significant visitors included local Congressman Harry Englebright and Department of Interior officials. Collins was able to cultivate an important network of people all related in some way to the fortunes of Lassen Volcanic. At the same time, he and his staff had to process an average of five hundred visitors a day, all intent on having their particular interests served.

By 1932 Walker Collins had managed to establish a core of facilities, a headquarters building, staff residences (including a superintendent's house), services and programs essential to the Park. Still, his budgetary problems continued and even worsened as the National Economic Depression set in. From 1933 on, Federal recovery programs, especially the "Emergency Conservation Work" (ECW) programs and the "Civilian Conservation Corps" (CCC), provided substantial physical labor and material supplies which ultimately overcame some of his NPS financial constraints (See Figure 3-2.) Through these "New Deal" agencies, Collins' ambitious infrastructure plans became ever more realizable: service roads, water systems, sewage systems, nature trails, campgrounds, picnic grounds and needed equipment. Park Headquarters in Mineral functioned as the administrative hub of all this activity, involving hundreds of personnel besides the regular park staff. Collins and his able Accountant, Wilbur Moore, had to juggle a variety of Federal accounts in meeting NPS-approved project demands. Budgeting from various agency accounts became standard practice, if not always strictly "correct" procedure.

Although he worked diligently to respond to visitor and user interests, Collins persisted in expressing his concept of a primitive, wild and scenic Park. He shared this interest with others and in his annual reports pointed out the natural attributes of Lassen and their educational values as its outstanding features. Based on the foundational work of his Park Naturalists, Farmer and Scherer, Collins wanted to expand the educational program in line with his physical plans. A national advisory committee on education, under NPS, regarded Lassen Volcanic Park as an ideal setting for a top-flight educational program and informed the

Superintendent of its expectations. All Walker Collins needed was adequate support from NPS leadership and Congress. But when he tried to get special funds for a model relief map of the Park, he was rebuffed. So he transferred funds from his own budget, selected an expert cartographer model-builder whose work he knew personally and produced an excellent model that was judged by professional peers as flawless. But NPS-Washington then chided him for not going through official channels. His top boss in Washington, Horace Albright, did not himself complain of financial shortages at this time. In fact, he reported that his budgets under the Hoover Administration were even on the increase in spite of the national depression.

In the area of commercial concessions in the Park, Collins proceeded cautiously and conservatively. The Drakesbad Resort was actually a guest ranch with a group of cabins and a hotel-restaurant in the Warner Valley's hot springs area. It had predated the Park's creation and was the only facility of its kind. It was owned and operated by the Sifford family, who had purchased the site in 1900 from Edward Drake. Although Drake had been a guide for visitors, the Siffords made the first trails and conducted the first hiking parties around Lassen. They were early supporters of the national park initiative along with their good friends the Rakers. The Siffords had hosted many prominent visitors long before 1916.

In 1933, Collins obtained approval for a second tourist concession at Manzanita Lake, just inside the northwest entrance. His idea was not to create a resort atmosphere, but rather something with natural simplicity and exposure to the indigenous environment. Natural tones were uppermost in his planning of the facility. Two park rangers, Don Hummel and Charles Keathley from Michigan, obtained financing from a Michigan friend (Dallas Dort of the General Motors family), and built a store and guest lodge in 1933. In the past, efforts had been made by major companies to establish a resort-type community rivaling that of Yosemite. But this more modest site became the core of future Lassen tourist accommodations. It complemented well the rustic campgrounds and wilderness trails, helping to maintain a natural, conservative air. This posture was in keeping with original NPS intentions and philosophy on the uses and preservation of park resources as well as with Collins' ethics.

The "Collins Affair"

After 1932, however, Collins encountered increasing difficulty in getting his budget approved. He repeatedly complained to Washington that his requests for more resources, including an adequate vehicle for headquarters, seemed to fall on deaf ears. He defended criticism of employees by submitting point-by-point rebuttals to NPS officials. He found himself forced to shift budgetary items around to suit the actual requirements he faced on a day-to-day basis. This practice included using his own money to help finance a new vehicle and adjusting his financial reports in a way to cover this expenditure.

During 1934 NPS dispatched investigators to Mineral Headquarters on a routine and customary fact-finding mission. They gave Collins and Accountant Moore a "clean bill of health" in regard to administrative and accounting procedures. Someone in Washington was not satisfied, however, and the next year further inquiries into Park business procedures were ordered. This time one of the investigators uncovered evidence of equipment purchases and the financing of the automobile with the use of unorthodox accounting methods, including use of private monies. Notwithstanding the fact that Superintendent Collins had received high praise in the past for his leadership and management record, some indiviudals or group seemed intent on "getting" Collins in one way or another. A strange incident may have provoked Washington's determination to do so, although no documented evidence of any connection between the two events has been found.

In January, 1935, one of the private inholders within park boundaries, Mrs. Nellie I. Supan, took a vengeful course of action. A relative of the late Mathias Supan, she operated with her son a concession located at the old "Sulphur Works." This facility was unapproved and unregulated by park administration but enjoyed protection by virtue of its location on a private inholding within park boundaries. Supan's heirs had insisted on exploiting mineral claims of unknown worth within the Park and adjacent to other geologically significant sites. The Supans also insisted on operating and expanding tourist concessions whose standards were questionable. This insistence irritated park officials.

Nellie Supan wrote a personal letter to President Franklin D. Roosevelt (See Figure 3-3.) This message was very derogatory to Walker Collins, who Mrs. Supan charged was a pro-Hoover man who "worked hard to get Hoover back." Collins and NPS had tried to persuade the Supan Family to cede their properties over to the Park, for just compensation. But discussions did not progress satisfactorily. NPS Director Hillary Tolson, to whom the Supan letter was first referred for reply, assured Mrs. Supan that Superintendent Collins was doing a fine job. He had been praised by NPS Director Horace Albright for submitting "the best plan" for park development he had ever seen. But someone in either the Interior

Secretary's office or in the White House underscored on Mrs. Supan's letter her references to Collins' alleged ties to former President Herbert Hoover.

In the meantime Department of Interior Secretary Harold Ickes, a close political ally and confidant of the President, had ordered the second investigation into Collins' administration of the Park. Ickes was well known for his demands for unscrupulous and "clean" performance by Federal employees. He was well aware of the corruption scandals that had rocked Washington during the 'twenties. The examination of park records led to the "revelations" about irregular accounting practices. These reports were used to substantiate Secretary Ickes' charges against Collins of malfeasance in office and of indebtedness to the U.S. Treasury. It would be another feather in Ickes' political hat. In a telegram received by Park Ranger Lester Bodine, on July 19, 1935, from NPS Director Tolson, Superintendent Collins was given five days to exonerate himself from all charges, or face dismissal. Ranger Bodine later stated, "I could not believe what I was reading on the ticker." While Walker Collins was composing in great detail replies to all charges, a second telegram from Ickes received on July 25 summarily dismissed the Superintendent without a fair hearing or review of his case. The shock reverberated throughout the Park, where morale had been high. Collins enjoyed great confidence among staff, colleagues and surrounding communities. Politics had struck its devastating blow in raw, open and brutal fashion.

This dastardly act had the same spirit of revenge and retribution that had struck down, sixty years earlier, the tribal dwellers trying to defend their sacred territory. Human hate has no cultural boundaries. Collins' record and his accomplishments, and the building of a park that promised to do justice to the mission of the National Park Service, went all for nought as he got caught in the vice of political vengeance and intrigue. The maneuverings of certain NPS officers and their efforts at undermining his staff now could be seen in a new light. The final blow was dealt by the "head man" himself, acting as it were in behalf of the President, the ultimate authority. We can assume, however, that the plot or plan had been prepared by one of his lieutenants in the NPS. (Figure 3-4, shows one of the top Washington bureaucrats, Arthur E. Demaray, who had come to the Park officially to install Collins' successor).

Walker Collins left his beloved Lassen Park a broken and disheartened man, taking a small post in another part of California far from Fire Mountain. This bureaucratic interference from outside the Park was the first of a series of crises in park managment perpetrated by external political maneuverings. It was a prime example of the contradiction between professional management of a national preserve, dedicated to realizing a human ideal, and political control over that management function, from points outside the domain itself. It was a classic example of a medieval political mentality operating in contemporary "civil" society, of persons unfamiliar with the realities of the park making absurd decisions or unfounded conclusions without due process or a simple hearing of the case. It would appear that Mr. Demaray fits such a description, if we take only his outward appearance as evidence, which hardly corresponds to that of a robust ranger.

The Collins case pointed to the need for a mechanism for screening out pernicious political intent, whatever its justification, and removing it from the decision-making process itself. The political process leading to a final decision or policy determination, ought to be free of personal bias. In his fourteen-year stewardship of Lassen Volcanic National Park, Walker Collins had sought to create such a logical, information-based process. He had appealed to Director Albright for minimum funds to build a good inventory of living organisms as well as geological features. Time and again he pleaded with NPS-Washington for rationality, for explanations of their decisions and clarification of goals. But his efforts were rebuffed by a political machine that circumvented even Mather and Albright, and prevented them from reaching their well-intentioned goals. NPS leadership in this case was negligent, leaving the organization open to decision-making by crass, "seat-of-the-pants" politics.

The issue of political bureaucracy and park management is a theme our story will return to later in this book. It is a continuing problem for career park people who seek to serve in ways consistent with a wholesome philosophy of park preservation and a dedication to high quality work. The "Collins Affair" stands, and is recalled by old-timers, as a most sordid chapter in Lassen Park development. This story shows how it had been preceded by a number of nagging problems perpetrated by NPS officials whose motives remained both obscure and unchallegeable. Federal bureaucrats, sitting far from the scenes of day-to-day park administration, made critical decisions without the benefit of first-hand knowledge or appreciation of on-site challenges or issues.

Stability and Maturity (1935 - 1955)

The post-Collins period saw the slow but steady development of programs and organization on the basis of Collins' fourteen years' dedicated work. The replacement for Park Naturalist Scherer was Dr. Carl Swartzlow in November, 1935, a geologist who received his doctorate at The University of Missouri. He continued and expanded Scherer's work, and immediately saw the need for a visitors center where the Park's educational mission could be more adequately pursued. His request for such funds was the first in what would be a repeat scenario over the next fifty years. Park Naturalist Swartzlow was an energetic and creative individual who gave Lassen's educational and interpretive programs a solid scientific basis. Except for several years during World War II, he remained at Lassen Volcanic until his retirement in 1946.

Because of increasing pressures from the recreational public, the Park's facilities for sports-minded visitors gradually increased. By 1940, under Superintendent John Preston, annual winter skiing was allowed in the vicinity of Sulphur Works. Lassen became the most popular winter sports attraction in Northern California, next to Lake Tahoe. This image further heightened another major contradiction: the issue of natural unimpairment versus visitor demands for "multiple use," a concept whose roots lay back in the Agriculture Department's philosophy about accessing natural resources in the public domain.

Park rangers could not control what occurred along park boundaries, nor within the private inholdings that existed before 1916. Logging operations still affected the habitats of wildlife in park areas adjacent to them, and they also disrupted sometimes the natural flow of streams as well as muddied their waters. Livestock continued to cause similar problems. Park officials' irritation with these disturbances increased their determination to deal with them in the degree that resources to do so became available from Washington and NPS regional budget procedures.

Similar kinds of park abuse occurred at the hands of some inholders, particularly in the Juniper Lake tracts in the southeast area of the Park. For example, in anticipation of the 1941 Christmas season, property owners by the name of Snell, and others to whom they sold forest lots, decided to harvest some Christmas trees. They brought in bulldozers to knock down silver spruce trees up to thirty feet tall, in order to cut off the top eight or ten feet. Park rangers were powerless to stop this desecration, but registered their firm disapproval by targeting such inholdings for future acquisition.

Substantial progress was made after World War II toward incorporating the larger inholdings, two of which merit special mention because of their size and economic impact. Drakesbad Resort took the name of its founder, Edward R. Drake, who had acquired some 400 acres as a homestead in the early 1880s from an unknown owner, according to the Plumas County assessor's office. Located in the beautiful Warner Valley about twenty miles from the town of Chester, this property was blessed with hot springs, a gently flowing stream and lush meadows, some of which were more marsh than meadow. Drake built up a small tourist trade based on his mineral bathhouse and beautiful landscapes. In 1900 he sold these properties to Alexander Sifford, a teacher from Susanville, who soon settled there permanently with his family. The Siffords expanded and improved the accomodations, drained swampland, built trails into the extensive hot springs and fumarole area (later called "Devil's Kitchen"), and established both a cattle herd and horseriding stables. This enterprise was the first real tourist facility in Lassen country, providing full accomodations to a paying public. For over fifty years the Siffords operated within park boundaries until an attractive offer led the heir, Roy Sifford, to sell in 1953 substantial holdings to NPS, while donating other extensive acreage to the Park as a goodwill gesture. This transfer greatly helped the Park to control its destiny, while reserving a smaller tourist facility inherited from the Sifford family to serve a particular clientele. This service includes up to this day horseback riding, the bathhouse and a hotel-restaurant complex. The Sifford "saga" and contributions to the Lands of Lassen are written up in a personalized style by the late Roy Sifford in his book, "Sixty Years of Siffords at Drakesbad".

Another major inholder transfer occurred with acquisition in 1952 of the famous, but also sometimes infamous, "Sulphur Works" facilities owned by the Supan family. The Supans had obtained a Federal patent giving them rights to exploit mineral deposits and to develop their land. The mineral aspect of the property proved to be of little real value. A few commercial ventures involving a service station, store and cabins were somewhat more rewarding. But the Supan property lay astride the main park road, a factor which caused both embarrassment and impediments to the superintendent's exercising full control over his domain. After several unsuccessful negotiating sessions, the issue went to federal court, which in 1952 gave the Supans a modest award in exchange for their property transfers and interests.

These and other acquistions greatly enhanced the internal coherence of the Park and provided both management and employees with more authority and control over the entire park domain. They helped bring the Park into its full maturity and size, insofar as federal negotiators in the Agriculture and Interior Departments had determined what its dimensions should be. These changes divested the Park of old appendages which harkened back to cultural and social values inconsistent with the national park ethic. With adequate resources, Lassen

Park might move more creatively into a new era of either multiple uses or return to genuine wilderness.

Both during and after World War II, parks' budgets generally suffered neglect in Washington, and the case of Lassen was compounded by an obstinate political pattern of disregard for some of its most basic needs. These neglects had negative affects on staff morale, and they were even more pronounced where poor housing was concerned. Dramatic changes were forecast, however, under the leaderhip of NPS Director Conrad ("Connie") Wirth.

Enjoying a good relationship with nature-loving President Dwight Eisenhower, Wirth and his colleagues drew up ambitious plans for a broadscale revamping of the national park system in a program entitled, "Mission 66." The plan was to invest heavily in both infrastructures and program development over a ten-year period, 1956 - 1966. (See Notes.)

The Mission 66 announcement sent park staffs across the country into frenzied planning work to attract Federal funds to their beleaguered parks. Lassen was no exception, and its superintendents during those momentous years (Freeland, Sylvester, and Moore) made valiant efforts to improve Lassen's conditions, status and mission. The next chapter tells the story of what happened to their dreams, which became embroiled in a series of disturbing political contradictions involving the Park's mission and resources.

3-1. Lassen Volcanic National Park (1939 boundaries).

3-2.   Civilian Conservation Corps Mess hall, Lassen Park (1935).

STAMP: Respectfully
referred for consider-
ation. (signed: Louis
McHenry Howe. Secy to
President.)

STAMP: Rec'd Office
of Interior Dept.
Secretary Feb. 5-1935

President Rosefelt

Dear Sir.

I am sending you birth day greetings
along with the mentioning my sons birth day on the 30th
day of Jan. he was born 1892 on that date and we named
him Adlai Stevenson Supan after the vice President under
Cleveland. we are all good democradts. We received the
patent on the Supan Sulphur Works. Now President Rosevelt
if you would do your self justice in the next election you
would get rid of L.W. Collins the Park Superintendent of

the Volcanic National Park. he and his men worked hard to

get Hoover back.

Yours Very Truly

Nellie I.Supan, Red Bluff

[Source: National Archives, RG-79, File 12-17, LVNP.]

3-3.   Nellie Supan's Letter to FDR.

3-4. NPS Assistant Director Demaray, Mrs. Demaray and
Acting Superintendent Townsend

CHAPTER 4

CONFLICTS OF POLITICAL CULTURE: BARONS AND VASSALS

Backgrounds to Conflict

The founding fathers of the national parks system, such as Stephen Mather, Horace Albright and Northern California Congressman Raker, were the "white knights" of the new *cause célèbre*, "Preservation." Imbued with an ideal and with a vision of the future, their concern focused on preserving for America's posterity as much of its grand wilderness areas as would be possible. And they expected that those magnificent domains would serve primarily to educate the public in the values of the nation's natural heritage, before urban-industrial culture would sweep them aside, just as it had already done to Native American cultures. (See Notes for studies on national parks and policies.)

It was not their intent that a national administration of parks and forests should advance political interests, both personal and partisan, ahead of the best interests of a national park or national forest. They expected that professional personnel, well qualified and knowledgeable about the character and requirements of park domain, would be able to manage a preserve in the best interests of conservation and preservation. Nor did they intend to favor policies that ran counter to enlightened elements in the communities supporting wilderness preservation, or seeking wholesome recreation. But these early visionaries unwittingly created a system of fiefs whose political jurisdiction lay with a cohort of barons, bureaucratic chiefs, who commanded a host of vassals charged with managing their fiefs.

At Lassen, this story shows how contention grew between the barons at central or federal level and their vassals, the park superintendents, who had direct charge of the fief. The Collins experience typified the unsavory quality of that relationship. Its nature and the sometimes bitter and insensitive actions by political chiefs against their underlings reveal something about national culture and character. Their worst expression had occurred even before the creation of a national bureaucracy in the outrageous annihilation of Lassen Indian cultures by posses condoned by the U.S. Army and the Bureau of Indian Affairs. In the Collins case, the U.S. Government's political bosses extinguished several careers for reasons of petty rivalries and personal prestige. There is a degree of parallel between the two kinds of political behavior.

Although the age of the automobile was dawning, the leaders of the national parks movement could not forsee the likes of the snowmobile, all-terrain vehicles, and huge power-driven ski lifts. But as public officials they were already exposed to the constant public pressures clamoring for various amusements within the parks. The spectacle of Yosemite in the mid-twenties was perhaps the best example of their yielding to popular fads. There, under park concessionaire Curry, NPS leaders condoned jazz musical festivals, a resort hotel and other sensate fare promoting a kind of "playboy-playgirl" atmosphere. As the official custodians, NPS leadership had to assume some responsibility for these departures from their original ideals and goals. Were they helpless?

All three of those national-parks advocates had, in the Muir tradition, much experience in the wilderness regions of the West. Albright was raised in the southern Sierra Nevada Mountains, which nurtured his values and feelings. Mather, a graduate like Albright of the University of California-Berkeley, was an avid backcountry buff who took groups into the wilderness to experience nature first-hand. For example, in 1915 he led a group of national political and institutional leaders into the Sequoia and Yosemite wildernesses to impress on them the grandeur and values of primitive America. None of those who hiked the trails and camped out with him were apt to forget them. Congressman Raker, with his family and friends, spent much leisure time in Lassen country, cultivating an intimate relationship with its many primeval attractions. They were the first advocates of making the region a national park. And they adored its beauties and primitiveness.

Unfortunately for aboriginal culture of the Lassen Indians, those national, and even state, leaders were quite unmindful of native values and heritage. This recognition would come much later. At this early, formative period, their lack of awareness of Native American ways deprived their philosophy and early policies on management, of a rich tradition in the very essence of preservation. Would NPS's first two decades have been different if it had been nourished by that aboriginal culture? The works of anthropologists like Kroeber, Waterman and Sapir were just beginning to bear fruit in publications. But these were not yet generally available beyond the professional circles producing them.

The power not only to create, but also to decide matters of detail and to administer national parks with professional management staffs and technical equipment, shifted increasingly to Washington. In the early 'thirties, "Regional Offices" across the country were established by NPS directors. Washington and the regionals began to decide issues that were not policy but essentially substantive, or matters of inherent concern only to local park managers. Decisions often became subject to purely "political" considerations. Whether or not they were actually resolved became secondary, viz. NPS meddling in park affairs during the Collins years.

The Collins tragedy was the first of a long series of such incidents which proved that the founding fathers' expectations were somewhat chimerical, if not ill-founded, with respect to political infighting, trade-offs and raw use of power. While the story tells of just one fine park, it is possible and tempting to surmise that the behavior of NPS barons and others was fairly consistent throughout the park system. In one sense, the very fate of Lassen Volcanic National Park was hung up in the vicissitudes and fortunes of political behaviors, postures and bargaining that most often had little to do with the real merits of the issues or policies surfacing at a particular time and in a particular park.

What the exact motives of this or that political personage or group were, is hard to pinpoint. Tracing the course of national and regional political struggles over control and use of the nation's natural resources, Samuel Hays shows how special interest groups, both for and against natural preservation, doggedly lobbied lawmakers to favor their cause. In his masterful book on the Muir legacy, Stephen Fox etches clear and sometimes dramatic images of the various interest groups and preservationist societies vying for control and influence over park governance. But each park is a special domain in its own right, and to understand it requires intimate detail of local circumstances. For Lassen, we can draw profiles of situations involving political actors, both the bureaucrats (barons) and managers (vassals), which illustrate contending forces and influences vying for control over the people's park. Lest we forget, the parks belong to the people, not to the barons. If the people act responsibly, perhaps they can expect to enjoy their parks in ways that nature and its requirements for preservation would dictate.

Every human organization, large and small, harbors zones of influence marking the extent or range of members' power or authority. These zones may result from logical processes of decision-making based on "hard" data (scientific information and experience), or from arbitrary use of authority based on political, personal ("good old boy") or other systems. Both can be seen as legitimate, but typically one kind of zone will be more reality based than another. The management of Lassen Park exhibits a goodly number of political profiles that enlilghten us about how decisions and goals get made and are imposed on a national park. One such profile deals with the role of park planning in NPS administration. (See Notes for main source.)

Planning for Protection and Natural Renewal: A Political Gamble

The NPS Mission 66 program raised high expectations among Lassen Park personnel. They had for almost thirty years hoped for an upgrading in the quality of park employee housing and facilities, and especially for an adequate visitors center, essential to conduct a quality educational program. In theory, all national parks were on similar footing in applying to NPS-Washington, through their Regional Office, for a fair share of the financial resources provided by appropriations for Mission 66. Master Plans must be coherent, demonstrate need, enjoy Regional Office support and be technically sound and feasible.

Many years before, Walker Collins had laid out not only excellent plans for Lassen's development, but also a set of criteria for sound planning work. In a memorandum to NPS-Washington, he stated: "In preparing the foundation for future park publicity and educational work, it is essential that authentic data be secured, written up and published on the geology, fauna, and botany of the park ...." His notion of scientific integrity had established at Lassen a precedent and a tradition of sound, responsible planning work. Professionals such as Scherer and Swartzlow carried forward this standard, and Lassen's staff down through the years has tried to adhere to this level of work.

During 1956-1963, several planning documents were drafted at Park Headquarters in Mineral. But only in July, 1963, did the Director of the Western Regional Office in San Francisco give his approval of a master plan. A strong theme running through the plan was restoration of natural conditions, along with containing and limiting visitor impacts. These ideas rang back to the basic concepts of the Collins years and reiterated early NPS emphasis on natural unimpairment.

Lassen's "Master Plan" never reached the Washington office, however. We have to conclude that in San Francisco the good old boys, sitting around the table of decision-making, had to find one or more sacrificial lambs if their personalized ranking of requests, referred to as "wish lists," for appropriations were to survive the axes of Federal bureaucrats and legislators. One NPS veteran offered the explanation that remote California parks like Lassen, far removed from wealthy urban areas and their skilled political brokers, do not fare well behind the closed doors of partisan authority and the brokering and horse-trading that goes on. Factors such as need, public service, scientific data, and sound planning do not compete with the hard facts of personal privilige, elite influences, favoritisms, personal loyalties and the joys of bargaining as practiced by the old pros. For many of them, showplaces and enjoyment offered at parks like Yosemite and Hawaii seemed more in keeping with their ideas of what a national park for the people should be. Such a park enjoyed wider public acceptance and garnered more political support for candidates for public office.

For those career pros, educating an ignorant public about volcanism and park ecology was comparatively unexciting and rather irrelevant. Even a romantic, dedicated chief administrator such as NPS Director Connie Wirth was not impermeable to the seductions of such political sophistry. For he knew personally how much Lassen needed an all-round upgrading, and in particular a visitors center. But he failed to intervene in Lassen's cause, abiding by the informal rules of the good old boys, the barony on which much of his own personal power depended.

Aside from a few projets such as sewer overhaul and extending electric power lines, Lassen Park did not cash in on Mission 66. Commenting on this near exclusion from Federal attention, Lassen Superintendent Hallock, the vassal, wrote a letter to his boss, the Western Regional Director: "In reviewing and studying the master planning, development schedules, and construction programs I am impressed with how little this park has benefitted from ... Mission 66 ..., both by comparison to other NPS areas and in relation to the needs of this area." If Mr. Hallock had used stronger language, perhaps he could have influenced NPS; but on the other hand, he might have also been reassigned to an even more remote little park. At Lassen he could at least enjoy its beauties and relative insularity. He had learned that such peace comes with a price. Vassals do not invite the barons into their foyer to brow-beat them.

Later superintendents fared no better. Even though staff at Lassen were among the first to anticipate wilderness legislation and come up with a realistic plan for natural resource preservation, their efforts were not rewarded by either San Francisco or Washington. The political riddle persisted. When in 1977 Lassen Park added a Natural Resource staff position, a program of scientific monitoring could ostensibly begin. But in comparing the awarding of research monies adequate for this specialist to conduct the needed research and monitoring work, we find that Lassen's budgets were woefully behind those of other parks. For example, the national volcanic park in Hawaii received much more generous attention in appropriations than did Lassen. Of course, it's more fashionable for NPS officials to visit Hawaii than to trek up to Lassen, with its primitive environment. In fact, as of 1990, the Western Region Director, Stanley Albright (nephew of Horace Albright) had never even visited Lassen Park! But his interest in volcanism had inspired him to conduct several field visits to Hawaii. Do taxpayers have a right to ask, why this discrepancy?

The history of repeated rejection by NPS and Congress of Lassen's most fundamental needs forms a pattern that approaches a pathology of sorts. Some veteran park employees at Lassen became almost paranoid about the very idea of neglect. One park naturalist confessed that Lassen's plight marked the most weird contortion he ever knew of public policy within the national park system, unscrutable and inexplicable. Another described it as a haven for those who withdraw from the competitive system and the environment of careerist ambitions that distorted even common-sense approaches to good park management. And still another said that Lassen is a hole to be avoided by anyone seeking a career future. But whatever the real reasons for Lassen's political misfortunes, this story nonetheless unfolds a pattern of strange, contradictory and persistent relationships. A beautiful park was condemned to mediocrity in terms of its capacity to fulfill its mission, as compared to its sister parks in California and most parks in the nation.

Lassen Volcanic's staff had to wait until 1981 for Regional approval of its second attempt at overhauling park facilities. But once again, the Director (Chapman) had to shelve it because, he said, the Park simply did not carry the political clout that would earn it the dollars required. He also referred to Lassen's remoteness and the failure of surrounding communities to pressure Congress. Finally, there came the Reagan Administration's cost-cutting agenda which grated against NPS needs in general. Political factors once more dashed Lassen employees' hopes for a new deal.

The Politics of "Problem Management"

The range of hot issues that Lassen superintendents have faced for over seventy-five years runs from rancher Kelly's cows mucking up Kings Creek meadows, to battles among interest groups over ripping up mountain slopes for ski lifts, to large corporations' sinking deep wells in search of new energy sources. And many more.

Walker Collins had tried all through his superintendency to get range cattle out of the Park. When he and his rangers posted no-trespassing signs along the boundary, the ranchers joked that their cows could not read. There were simply not enough rangers to patrol the boundaries. In some range land next to the National Forest, Collins was obliged to issue grazing permits for small fees which brought in a few extra dollars. On occasion the number of cattle reached threatening proportions, and meetings between staff and ranchers became heated. But NPS-Washington never became so concerned about this problem that it sought funds to implement a firmer policy of control. Some career park folks feel that the U.S. Department of Agriculture has always carried a lot more weight in Washington than has the Interior Department. Such was the case during World War II, when the need for beef and the scarcity of manpower were arguments used to overlook the issue of livestock in park pastures. But the problem persists even today, and Lassen rangers admit that some cattle still enjoy the privacy of lush meadows in Lassen Park. The Kelly boys have the final laugh after all, for their ranch still prospers today.

A somewhat thornier and more publicized issue has been horseback riding in the Park. Before the construction of roads, travel by horseback was necessary for park patrol and assistance to stranded visitors. That practice was a concession to the principle that horses, not being indigenous animals, had no rightful place within the Park. They not only damaged trails intended for human feet but also excreted dung carrying seeds from grasses grown far from mountain vegetation. As such, horses' impacts ran squarely counter to the policy of unimpairment.

The strong tendency to admit horses was partly historical precedent and partly the avid enthusiasm and influential nature of the horseriding society in California. Park horses were still used until about 1960, and thereafter phased out. But recreational use is a horse of another color. During the 1980's, horseback parties were on the increase in Lassen Park. The Sifford family's popular rustic resort included stables and offered trails in Warner Valley and then up into adjacent wilderness trails. Mr. Roy Sifford, the guest ranch owner, felt that Rangers' concern for over-doses of horse manure was "much ado about nothing." This example was sufficient for California associations such as the "Backcountry Horsemen of California" to demand wider and less restricted access to the trails.

The wilderness use plan restricted both the number of horses and routes to be allowed. Applying these restrictions to horseback parties faced the small ranger contingent with an almost impossible enforcement task. Furthermore, the park superintendent came under direct pressure from one of the ranking Western Region officials, Associate Director Lew Albert, himself an avid horseman, to be lenient toward his friends. To him it was apparently a small matter that horses grazed in restricted meadows, leaving behind their copious droppings, or broke down trail shoulders, or waded where they wanted, muddying and polluting ponds and streams. Fingerling trout could hardly survive under such conditions. If horse parties were reminded of such violations (when they were rarely caught), their responses were sometimes indignant. R. H. Cochran, head of the Backcountry Horsemen Association angrily wrote Superintendent Gilbert Blinn, railing against "restrictive regulations": "I think it is time for a change.... Your policies include such archaic requirements that riders must always stay and remain on the trail...." Mr. Cochran preferred depositing horse dung in meadow and stream to respecting nature's fragile laws and relationships, about which he either knew little or cared less. After this incident, horse parties continued as before to enjoy their particular style of wilderness use. Barons rode herd on the vassals, and got their way. At this point in America's historic battle for environmental preservation, such behaviors appear childish and immature. Those who behave so are sad examples for our children's future guidance.

Building the "Big Sliding Board"

A still more sensitive issue, and one that involved a much larger public constituency, was winter sports. In the early days skis were essential for rangers to move around during winter. A few major ski events were staged during the 1930's, and a small ski tow was installed next to Sulphur Works in 1934. NPS officials resisted opening up the Park to large numbers of winter recreationists, but some concessions were made just prior to World War II. During 1938-41, Superintendent Preston negotiated with NPS-Washington for a modest expansion of what he called "one of the finest skiing areas" in California. Organizing his own advisory committee on the matter, Preston garnered support from several skiing associations, chambers of commerce, the press, and even the Sierra Club in support of expansion. In this case the vassal went on the offensive and convinced the barons, notably NPS Acting Director John White, to help defray expenses of a larger Sulphur Works ski operation. Associate Director Demaray followed suit with approval of constructing some new facilities to accomodate skiers. Sleds and toboggons were banned, however, at Preston's recommendation.

As major activities skiing and then later snow-mobiling were not serious threats to the Park's landscapes until the 1950s and especially 'sixties. And public demands by Northern Californian fun-seekers for more facilities steadily increased. By the mid-fifties, ski facilities were expanded at a new location, near the Park's south entrance station, with several tows in operation. Five hundred skiers could be accomodated. In 1965, a structure called the ski chalet was built at this new site with a parking lot that could accomodate 650 persons and about 200 cars. The total number of winter sports enthusiasts reached 17,000 per season. Instrumental in bringing about this radical change in park policy were local Congressman Clair Engle, chambers of commerce in the valley towns and sportsmens' associations. The nature ethic of unimpairment had gone down the drain, and the power of the purse weighed more heavily than ever before in NPS policy decisions.

Reactions from other politically active quarters were soon felt. Reflecting the influence of naturalists like Aldo Starker Leopold (the late professor at The University of Wisconsin), and the "heirs" of John Muir, founder of the Sierra Club, an environmentalist movement mounted counter arguments and pressures. Their efforts helped in getting the 1964 Wilderness Act through Congress, which laid out a program of preserving vast tracts of land still in the natural state, and of reclaiming others which could perhaps be salvaged. Lassen figured among those having extensive wilderness areas.

While the Park's staff worked steadily ahead on a wilderness plan, the lobbyists and supporters of major ski facilities and of snowmobiles made headway also. A California concessioner, "U.S. Natural Resources, Inc.," received NPS approval in 1970 to expand facilities to accomodate 1,200 skiers per hour, with a vertical elevation of 1,025 feet. Although the firm's plan stated that the new chair lift would not affect "the environment or the ecology of the ... region adversly," it gave no evidence of what impacts might occur. It failed to account for archeological sites on grounds bearing vestiges of Native American cultures. These were later recognized by park specialists who altered plans so as to avoid their desecration. Congressman Howard "Bizz" Johnson was a main backer of the ski operation, and his influence reached the desks of engineer-designers at the NPS Denver Service Center, responsible for final technical specifications in park development. An official there recognized that Johnson and NPS Director Hartzog had reached a "personal agreement," which he termed an "informal understanding," on the ski expansion projects. The barons remained firmly in the saddle, and winter recreation programs at Lassen became a permanent fixture in the Park's development. Vassals bowed heads.

The surrounding communities in Northern California were split, however, over this planned massive increase. Environmental proponents remained active, publicizing their views favoring protection of environmental and wilderness resources and either the containment or phase-out of winter sports. By the late 1970's, top echelons in the Interior Department now leaned toward preservation, as opposed to economic development and the Secretary's Advisory Committee recommended a phase-out of Lassen's downhill skiing operations. But NPS career persons found means to follow neither public opinion nor Interior's advice. Western Region Director Howard Chapman "voted" for a 2,000 foot triple chairlift mechanism, hung on cables supported by huge steel towers anchored in massive concrete footings. Park records show no substantive basis for Chapman's decision. Was it out of his love for skiing, or his willingness to serve the business community? Records reflecting the decision-making process and exchanges of information on this case either were never kept, or they did not find their ways to official files.

Some informal exchanges, however, between NPS planners and Congressman Johnson indicate fairly well the basis on which the ultimate decisions, which took effect in 1980-81, were cut. The "Denver Service Center" of NPS provided most of the technical work and project drafts for the national parks. At that preparatory stage the basic thrusts of park development were set, around which the various interested parties spun their webs of influence. On the Lassen ski proposal, one of the key project designers, Kenneth Raithel, had been reached by Congressman Johnson. Raithel responded favorably. In a handwritten note to a DSC colleague, he stated: "Re: the LAVO [Lassen Park] ski area, I found out that Harold 'Bizz' Johnson is its chief champion. Right or wrong, he has been a good friend of the Service in Congress, & I understand he and Geo. H. [Harzog] have an 'informal understanding.'" (Initialed R., for Kenneth Raithel). As far as the staff at Lassen, the community preferences, and the good of the Lands of Lassen were concerned, the deal had been already set. NPS Chief Hartzog, the Congressman with his political networks, and Regional Director Chapman had their ducks all in a line. There would probably be additional public input through hearings, but that voice would not have a real vote at the bargaining table. Had they been able to sit at the table, they would have had no chips to play with and the other players each knew what was in their partner's hand. The deal had been cut. Vassals again bowed heads to barons.

Park Superintendent Bill Stephenson (1974-1985) felt that this ski expansion was modest, for it maintained the ski operation, as he put it, "as it is now, a small family-oriented operation," pending construction of a major facility outside the Park. Whether a visitor count of between 20 - 30,000 per winter season represents a "family" kind of sport could be debated. At least the financing of the new structure, in the amount of four and a-half million dollars, would come largely from private funds. Yet the public has the right to ask if an investment of this magnitude could win the influence and vote of the NPS barons. In this case, was the Park a winner or a loser? It depends on what kind of card game you play.

The Government would finance revamping the chalet to make it more accomodating to larger crowds. The ski communities were delighted. No one consulted the flora, fauna, and fish what they thought of the consequences of this major change in environment. For a time, some park specialists felt that the Peregrin Falcon, known to inhabit the Park, might be molested by the cables. A post-study examination proved negative in this respect. Chapman dismissed other protective devices for the falcon as not even worthy of consideration. The baron's word was law, notwithstanding any evidence or reasoning to the contrary coming from career naturalists in the park service.

NPS engineers advocated a 2,100 foot triple chairlift system, to be anchored to steel towers set in large concrete footings. Extensive soil, tree, rock, and shrub removals were necessary for this large apparatus. No requirements as to pre-construction study of the affected terrains were stipulated, notwithstanding the knowledge that Native American summer camp sites had once been in the area. The developer and concessioner for the ski operation, John Koeberer, finally succeeded in 1981 to have his wish. He was not insensitive at all to environmental issues and cultural heritage, and his company vowed to abide by all existing laws and regulations governing these matters. At the same time, he was convinced that the recreating public, who "also pays taxes," has every right to use the Park as does any other user, such as the nature lover not needing mechanical thrills to enjoy Fire Mountain's many wonders. Information he failed to consider related to preservation of natural and cultural resources, which belong to all the people, not just to recreationists.

Following the ski station's "face lift," the profitability of the concessioner's winter sports gradually declined to a point that, by 1987, both NPS and the operator seriously considered phasing it out and eventually moving to another location. Apparently the forward planning skills and marketing analyses performed by those involved, from Denver to San Francisco to Washington, and back down to the Park itself, left a lot to be desired. "Much ado about nothing?" In the end, the environmentalists, Native American archeological sites and the cause of Lassen's overall environment stood to win, but at a considerable cost to both the cultural and natural endowment, which could not be restored exactly as it had been prior to development. One sport that did experience firm rejection by all decison-makers, however, was snowmobiling. It was banned in 1981.

The Twelve-million Dollar Hole

The politics of development took a precipitous lurch in the late 'seventies when Federal policies favoring alternative energy sources encouraged some companies to try ambitious, and sometimes questionable, explorations. One such venture occurred adjacent to Lassen Park, in a tract of land, known as "Section 36" (Tract No. 01-131), owned by a group of investors-developers called the "Andrus Trust 2." This inholding lay close to a very active thermal springs and fumarole area of the Park, high-lighted by Terminal Geyser. Some geologists and energy researchers believed that extensive thermal energy could be generated by sinking deep wells into this area. Because the company, Phillips Petroleum, Inc., kept its records private, we do not know exactly how seriously its engineers believed in the likelihood of striking large thermal domains whose steam was convertible into mechanical energy. Phillips first bored a hole 1,285 feet deep in 1962, and then capped it, presumably for future use.

Since the original legislation establishing the National Park Service and Lassen Volcanic Park in 1916 provided for the U.S. Reclamation Service to issue permits "to enter upon and utilize for flowage or other purposes any area" within a park for project development, Phillips Petroleum employed this statutory provision to access thermal areas. (Cf. US 39 Stat. 442, 1.) Mineral rights seemed to be accessible to private agencies. A 1930 statute, however, removed that provision and "the use of public lands in relation thereto." (Cf. US 46 Stat. 222.) Furthermore, the Thermal Leasing Act of 1970 also appeared to preclude thermal exploration on park lands, or in adjacent areas which could threaten a park's integrity.

In October, 1977, the local Plumas County Zoning Administrator issued a permit to Phillips, as "lessee to Andrus Trust, property owners," to resume drilling at the 1962 well head. Although there had been a recent public hearing in the Quincy Courthouse about drilling, attended by a Phillips official and the Park Superintendent, there was no indication that further exploration was in fact contemplated. The County Government did not inform the Superintendent nor the Regional Office in San Francisco about the negotiations leading to issuing the permit. If the drilling were to lead to marketable thermal energy, Plumas County would be sure to benefit. Park managers found out about the drilling only by pure accident when a park employee doing trail work in August 1978 heard the commotion and "went over to see what was going on." He reported the incident to park headquarters, and officials from Mineral visited the site the next day.

When asked by what authority the company was drilling inside park boundaries, the foreman said his orders "came from Washington," and he was prepared to "go to 4,000 feet." Park Superintendent Stephenson got on the phone to speak with Phillips executives in Salt Lake City. Their "Drilling Supervisor," Art Rolds, told Stephenson that he wasn't concerned about park policies and would continue drilling, even if Stephenson were to issue a "declaration of taking" in accordance with Federal law. Phillips Petroleum was clearly well protected in Washington and perhaps also in San Francisco's Regional Office.

Following the 1977 local hearing, the Director of NPS, William Whalen, had in fact addressed a request for a "declaration of taking" to the U.S. Senate Committee on Energy and Natural Resources on December 23, 1977. This Committee approved the request on January 9, 1978. The Secretary of Interior, Cecil Andrus, however, failed to forward the necessary NPS documents to the House and Senate Committees on Appropriations for the required budgetary action. These papers were retained at Interior until October 10, 1978. Meantime, the drilling operations had gone full steam ahead. Extensive disruption of the environment occurred around the well, which sat on a concrete pad and in a clearing the size of a football field, cut out in the middle of virgin forest land. Trees were felled, soil was removed and pushed aside, drainage ditches were dug creating "seas of mud," and the natural zone near Terminal Geyser got a face lift. All for "free?"

Park Superintendent Stephenson discussed the violations with Regional Director Chapman in September, 1978, and sought counsel about issuing a declaration of taking. Although Chapman reported to NPS-Washington that severe damage was being done to the park environment, he told Stephenson that his Washington bosses were "reluctant to take action," and that Whalen could not seem to locate the proper Phillips executive with power to halt the drilling! Besides, said Chapman, the drilling had already gone its course and the "damage was done." The delaying action by the Interior Department in Washington had given the oil company the time it needed to do its job. The legal authority for actually issuing a declaration of taking lay in fact with the park superintendent: the law empowered him to have the drilling operation closed down. But in the reality situation of "chain of command," Stephenson would not act alone and risk the heat of his Regional and Federal barons. As a good boy and vassal, he must obey or have his own toy guns taken away.

A still more interesting feature of this political game came in the aftermath of the drilling. The exploration came out "negative" in terms of commercially valuable thermal energy resources. Phillips Petroleum and the Andrus Trust group had spent sizable amounts of money in violation of Federal law and spoiled a significant tract of land within the Park's boundaries. Although congressional investigation was made on site, no criminal actions were forthcoming. Once this threshold was passed, both the oil company and the Trust petitioned the U.S. Government for "reparations" which they claimed were due for their efforts in seeking new energy sources valuable to the national economy, and to cover the land value lost to the Trust by cession of Section 36 (566 acres) to the National Park Service by means of its declaration of taking.

Phillips Petroleum received $992,000 in payment covering its expenditures, and the Andrus Trust got over $11 million in compensation! The American people got a messed up piece of park land and no real assurance that at some future time another energy explorer would come along and engineer a similar deal at taxpayer expense. The complete records about this rather sordid story have yet to be located and explored for all its ramifications. We do not know, for example, what transpired among the top officials both in NPS and in the Secretary of Interior's office, leading to a price of $19,000 per acre of undeveloped forest land. Were there favors involved between Phillips and government people for the long delays in bringing about appropriate government action? The "declaration of taking" was in fact delayed until April, 1980, when Superintendent Stephenson issued his order ending control by the Andrus Trust. In discussions with attorneys for Phillips Petroleum, a Lassen Park official said they told him that NPS and park managers behaved "just the way they had expected," so as to delay any formal action till the "show was over." If the Lassen tribes were to pass judgment on these doings, their verdict might have been: man is false, but Nature does not tell a lie.

Information obtained from former Interior Secretary Cecil Andrus, sheds no light on the mystery. But as Interior Secretary, his official role was limited to a public statement to assure the media and the American people that his Interior Department was a true defender of the national parks: "The National Park Service is in the process of assessing the impacts from this type of activity, ... and will pursue the protection of those unique park features to the legal limits of its authority." (November, 1978.) The statement reflects the heights of hypocrisy, since Phillips Petroleum and the Andrus Trust had already assured themselves of the conditions necessary to seek large compensations for their efforts and property redemption. Also, the formal Congressional "investigation" proved to be a whitewash of the entire messy affair.

The Manzanita Lake Affair

Nestled in the northwestern corner of Lassen Park is a scene of prime natural beauty rivaling that of any in our national parks: Manzanita Lake. Nestled near towering Lassen Peak, its shores graced by mixed woods of pines and aspens, the placid waters of this small lake reflect hieroglyphs of color, form, and motion in all seasons of the year. Close by, another beautiful body of water, "Reflection Lake," harbors similar attractions and, a little further into the woods, "Lily Pond" lies quietly, nostalgically shaded most of the day by stately conifers surrounding it. This unique ensemble of natural gems early attracted campers who came to enjoy its tranquil beauties and, often enough, to fish in the lakes. As new arrivals, these people, some of whom became permanent settlers, dislodged the Native Americans, the Atsugewi tribes, who had used the area for at least a thousand years.

This spot became the target of some enterprising individuals, the most prominent of whom was Benjamin Loomis and his family. He built a stone house there and became a strong supporter of the region's nationalization. Later entrepreneurs established a small concession offering tourist accomodations, supplies and recreation. The largest campground in the Park lay within walking distance of the "resort" which accomodated hundreds of visitors by the 1950's. The general quality of the campground and services available to tourists left much to be desired, however, and park planners urged NPS to grant funds adequate to serve the public. These demands (1972) included a modern visitors center, to replace the antiquated Loomis Museum, whose construction included porous lava rock which caused humid, inhospitable conditions for both humans and museum collections. Adequate facilities for interpretation and exhibits were essential to carry out the Park's educational mission. None of these requests were granted by the Government. Dr. Carl Swartzlow had made such a request thirty years earlier.

Unrelated at the time to the Park's neglected state was a geological formation connected with the Manzanita Lake region: "Chaos Crags." This lava upcropping at the base of Lassen Peak was of recent origin. About three hundred years ago the Crags let loose a massive rock avalanche which, riding on a cushion of compressed air, swept across the area adjacent to the Lake and deposited sufficient rock to dam Manzanita Creek, thus forming the lake itself. The geological research of Dr. Howell Williams had noted this relationship, but no further consideration was given the fact that only about 25% of the original mass of Chaos Crags was still there on the mountain. And no geological evidence appeared that pointed to the likelihood that this small remaining mass could repeat the previous event. (Figure 4-1.)

In the late sixties, however, a U.S. Geological Survey team investigated the Chaos Crags area and concluded that Manzanita Lake lay in a "hazard zone." Any future park development for tourists should occur beyond the zone demarcated as hazardous, or at least be so arranged that visitors use "sites of least risk." This report became subject to various interpretations both inside the National Park Service, and beyond. The scenario was designed for conflict.

Whether or not the Manzanita Campground and the private concessions should be closed, phased out or relocated became controversial. The user-public clammored for continued use of the site with as little physical change as possible. Park staff was more or less split on the issue, seeking a solution that would allow future development of a major visitors center and revitalized museum. A few challenged the official NPS interpretation of the geologists' report, which tended to dramatize the findings to a point that called for closure of the entire ensemble of facilities at Manzanita Lake. In fact, Regional Director Chapman repudiated counter arguments coming from competent observers and had Lassen Park Superintendent Dick Boyer transferred when he insisted that Lassen's latest development plans, including revitalization of Manzanita Lake, be funded.

Boyer's successor Murphy had at first no better luck, although many new technical opinions minimized the actual danger to the campgrounds where most people concentrated. Then commercial interests and community sentiment brought congressional pressure from Representative Johnson, who wanted to resolve the dilemma. For a moment it seemed if perhaps Lassen would get its development plans aproved after all. Some concessions had to be made on physical location of overnight camping and lodging, however, and Johnson also got a promise from NPS that a major ski operation would be built. This latter point seemed to be the main object of the "horse-trading."

A "fly in the ointment" then appeared in the concessioner's reluctance to relocating, due to costs, unless of course NPS would foot the bill. In a sense he was holding NPS hostage: meet my terms or we'll go out of business and, if we do, we'll seek compensation! Although Director Chapman had decided to agree with Congressman Johnson and go along with redevelopment, the concession issue and its looming cost opened the door for return to his original position: No major development at Lassen. The ostensible and publicized reason for his decision to close out ALL Manzanita Lake facilities permanently, was "geological hazard." The "real reason" was apppaarently the termination of the private concession, which required a sizable financial settlement by NPS. Once again, the U.S. Government came to the rescue of private parties, as had been the case with the thermal energy debacle. Politics prevailed over reality. The losers, once again, were John Q. Public and the professional park service staff at dear Old Lassen, and of course Fire Mountain itself. To this day, there is no visitors center worthy of the name at Lassen Volcanic National Park. Fifty years ago, Park Naturalist Carl Swartzlow might have predicted this. And the ghost of Walker Collins would observe that the vassals can't beat the barons at their game, unless they hold the deck in their own hands.

This series of political vignettes demonstrates a consistent theme: the inherent interest of Lassen Volcanic National Park, as a national preserve and heritage, represented by professional staff and a park manager ostensibly in position to lead them in pursuit of that interest, always succumbs to the interest of politically motivated bureaucratic agents at Regional and Federal levels. Our story tells us that there is no truly logical, scientific, and professional approach for park management in the National Park Service, as it applies to Lassen Volcanic National Park. The two echelons of administrative behavior are inherently at odds. The goals of the park, defined in situ, are at variance with the goals of the hierarchy, defined by self-interest, careerism and political survival. This profound contradiction is probably a characteristic, to some degree, of every national park and in many other domains of government. How are the public interests to be served, and how can the memory and vestiges of Native American culture be preserved?

MARGIN OF
CHAOS JUMBLES

MARGIN OF CHAOS
JUMBLES

REFLECTION LAKE

MANZANITA
LAKE

EXISTING
DEVELOPMENT
MANZANITA LAKE
LASSEN VOLCANIC NATIONAL PARK

NORTH

0   300
FEET

Nº 1200075
PC | JAN 76

UNITED STATES DEPARTMENT OF THE INTERIOR
NATIONAL PARK SERVICE

1   FIVE CABINS
2   CEDAR CABINS
3   BUDGET CABINS
4   DORMITORY
5   LODGE - DINING ROOM
6   MANAGER'S RESIDENCES
7   STORE - SNACK COUNTER
8   GAS STATION
9   CAMPER SERVICE STORE
10 RANGER OFFICE
11 ENTRANCE RESIDENCES
12 SUMMERTOWN RESIDENTIAL AND
    MAINTENANCE AREA
13 LOOMIS MUSEUM
14 REFLECTION LAKE NATURE TRAIL
15 LILY POND NATURE TRAIL
16 REFLECTION LAKE PICNIC AREA
17 MANZANITA LAKE PICNIC AREA
18 SWIMMING AREA
19 ENTRANCE STATION
20 AMPHITHEATER
21 CAMPGROUND
22 SEWAGE TREATMENT
23 WATER INTAKE
24 HISTORIC TRAIL

120 CAMPSITES
TEMPORARILY REOPENED
IN 1974

SERVICE ROAD

SURFACED ROAD

ROAD OPEN TO PUBLIC
TEMPORARILY

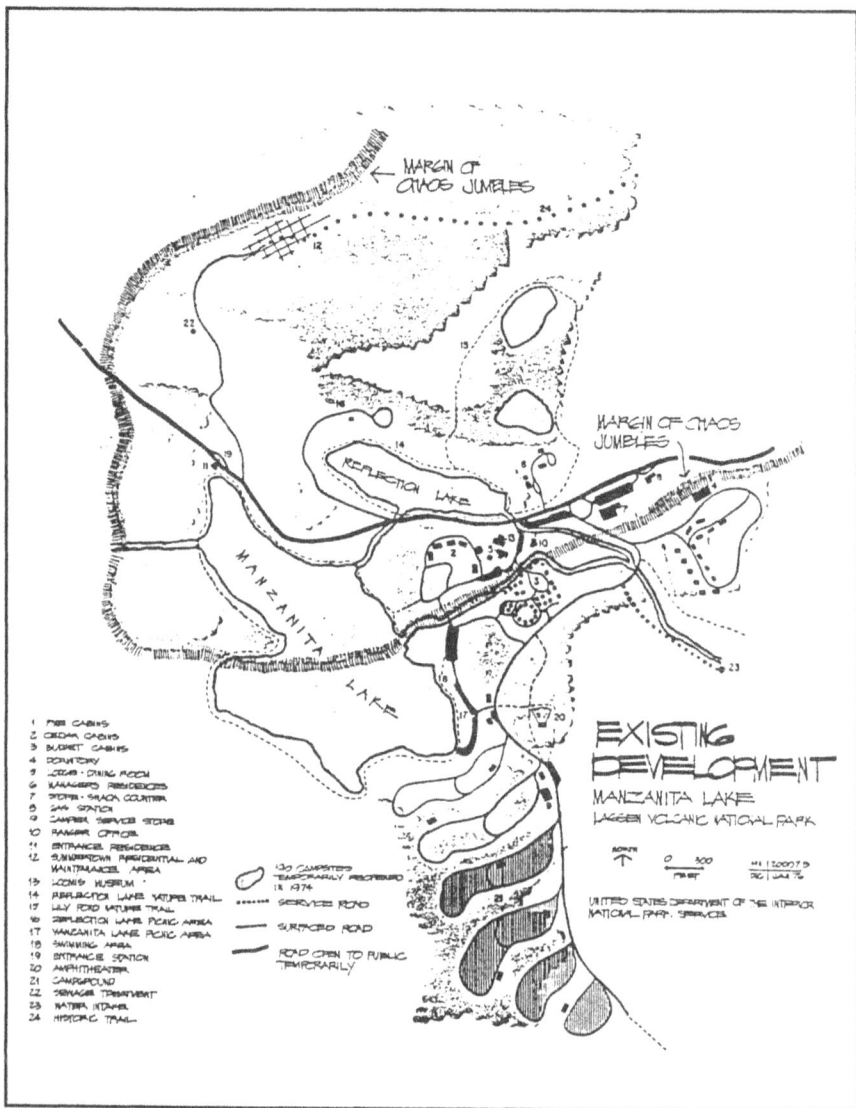

4-1.   Limits of Chaos Craigs Avalanche Area.

CHAPTER 5

THE PARK AS A SCHOOL OF LIFE: EDUCATION
VS. RECREATION

Introduction

Are these two concepts, education and recreation, mutually exclusive or inherently opposed to each other? Pedagogical theory says "no." But learning and recreating can interrelate, reinforce each other and jointly enrich the human experience. What links them together is the similarity of goals and purposes. One of the National Park Services' early and essential aims was that a national park should provide a rich educational experience for visitors, a place for the "scientist and student of nature," ... and for "those who would use their minds and hearts to know what God had created " as Horace Albright once said. Little, however, was said about recreation as a major purpose, the 1916 Act simply mentioning the concept of "enjoyment" as one of the purposes of natural preservation. Early NPS directors like Albright and Arno Cammerer, in particular, urged strict limitations on introducing mechanical contrivances into the parks simply for visitor comfort and convenience. By implication, this meant limiting sports-related machinery designed only for thrills and pleasures alien to the natural endowments.

For the aboriginal Americans, interacting with nature in all its forms provided an inescapable educational experience for families, in addition to learning survival skills. Their practical understanding and mastery of the plant and animal life around them and their knowledge of the phenomena of weather and seasons, gave them a very reliable information system for everyday living. Native reverence of and respect for all their natural surroundings, even the fish and game they took, penetrated all learning processes and apprenticeships. We recall the observation that Ishi, the Yahi stone-age man, made with respect to what is real knowledge: "Nature is always true."

The European-American, however, arrived with a very different attitude toward nature and its resources. The typical newcomer wanted to know first, how much of this or that resource could be used for personal and commercial purposes.

Most of them also saw wilderness as a unique opportunity for unrestricted fishing and hunting. However, by creating the national park the Government settled, at least in principle, the issue of material exploitation for personal gain. Most of the central mountain range was safe from economic development. Some elements of the white population then began gradually to approach Lassen Country with a new view to experiencing and understanding natural and geological phenomena, but largely from a background of urban, materialistic culture.

The Lassen tribal peoples always had strong recreational interests. Swimming, racing, hiking, hunting, fishing, field "hockey" and nature appreciation were pursuits they enjoyed as recreation. For the Native American, those activities had also a profound social intent of both bonding the members of tribal units and villages together, and releasing tensions built-up by close living quarters and occasional stress. Their reliance on individual human effort and personal skills contrasted sharply with white peoples' emphasis on machinery and external energy for satisfying their leisure as well as economic interests. In one way or another, all the recreational activities of the native people related to human survival as well as to social-psychological outlets.

Meanwhile, once the course toward natural preservation instead of economic exploitation had been set by U.S. public policy, a bridge had to be forged for bringing outside visitors, who were typically urban in background, into meaningful relationships with this primitive natural world. This task required that whatever economic pursuits might still be allowed within the Park must harmonize with the NPS-defined purposes of education and recreation. While in the early years the educational mission loomed foremost in the minds of park managers and employees, the recreating public soon became formidable competitors for the use of park resources, including time and personnel. The efforts by park administration to weld together programs that provided beneficial interactions between these two pursuits are basic to understanding the Park as an educational experience.

So we need to "take a ride" on the learning circuits developed at Lassen Volcanic National Park. Our story will explore also the issues arising from the Park's dual mission. (See Notes for sources.)

Foundations of Park Education

Lassen's alpine and volcanic features provided a wealth of opportunities for human learning about natural history and processes. Its cultural resources could have also been major assets had the tribal peoples not been so overwhelmingly crushed, and vestiges of their cultures swept away. Initially, Federal legislation establishing the Park and the NPS provided no philosophical framework for developing educational programs and the few directives for guiding staff work were meagre.

During the years 1880 - 1920, some of the early pioneers, such as the Sifford and Loomis families, and leadership from Forestry Supervisor Louis Barrett, developed some rudimentary programs for the nature-loving tourist. Their viewpoints as well as appeals for creating a national park circulated in local newspapers. This information provided the public with some degree of knowledge and impressions. A local citizen, Dr. Charles Goethe, advocated programs for educating the public before Ranger Walker Collins was able to issue leaflets with rules and suggestions about visiting various sites, after 1922.

Once NPS officials from Washington took the time to visit the Park, it became evident to them that its educational resources were substantial. Director Stephen Mather made the trip in 1926, accompanied by U.S. Congressman Temple. Two years later, the NPS Education Committee made a strong recommendation supporting an ambitious educational program at Lassen, stating that it "presents an exceptional possibility for development of a fully balanced and adequate educational program." A kind of blue ribbon group of leading lay persons, the Committee was headed by John C. Merriman, President of the Carnegie Institution of Washington. Its recommendations carried significant weight in the public mind. However, the arena of Washington politics and bureaucratic organizations presented another kind of challenge for NPS policy and park operations. In this respect Lassen is a reasonable test case for checking out how well the recommendations of an ostensibly non-political body such as the Education Committee might be realized in practice.

The Committee recommended that scientific personnel be charged with data collection that would establish a knowledge base for educational programs and for the general development of parks. The role of the park naturalist would occupy the key position in this approach, supervising scientific activities and managing the production of studies, research and publication. The Committee further indicated, with no reservations, the importance of that post in recommending a salary for the naturalist equivalent to that of the superintendent. Educational and related programs should not, the Committee cautioned, disturb the natural environment, which ought to be "retained as nearly as possible in its primitive condition."

It endorsed learning methods that made extensive use of hands-on kinds of experience. This meant that educational programs ought to emphasize direct

91

contacts by the visitor with natural phenomena, as opposed to dependence on verbal and written forms of communication. The aim was to promote personal, individualized experiences with natural realities, and to generate in the visitor a spirit of inquiry, reflection and inductive thinking. In educational circles this pedagogical theory was termed "sense realism," and "experiential learning," which were in vogue in America and in some parts of Europe at the time. Interestingly, native Americans had used this approach as their method of "instruction."

These broad criteria, while somewhat more philosophical than scientific in character, called for highly qualified park naturalists as educational leaders and a scientific knowledge base as the key elements in program development. Here were two essential criteria for future educational services in the Park.

Field visits by members of this Committee were followed shortly thereafter by a visit in 1929 of the new NPS Director, Horace Albright, a longtime associate of Stephen Mather, who had just died. Albright's enthusiasm for Lassen's potential led to his recommendation that Superintendent Collins embark without delay on a set of educational programs. Among his and the Committee's recommendations was the expectation that beautiful sites, such as Warner Valley and the area around the Drakesbad resort, should be preserved as nearly as possible in their primitive states. These conditions would enhance the educational values of the Park and its restorative mission.

In 1927, Benjamin Loomis and his wife had dedicated a Museum at Manzanita Lake for the Park's archeological specimens and other memorabilia, including Mr. Loomis' fabulous photographic collection on the 1914-15 eruptions. Along with the building, they deeded over to the Park a substantial amount of land to be incorporated within park boundaries. Since 1926, the Park also boasted a seismograph, operated by The University of California's Geology Department.

Collins and his rangers had worked steadily on trail-building leading to a number of sites, such as the hot springs at "Bumpass Hell," "Devil's Kitchen" (which had actually been done by the Sifford operation at Drakesbad), Mount Harkness, where the Park's third fire lookout station was constructed, and other accessible places. He also contracted with the California State Fish and Game Department to stock the streams and lakes with trout for anglers. The early settlers and sportsmen had ravaged most of those waters, all "in sport."

In line with unimpairment, Collins advocated that the main appeal of Lassen Volcanic Park lay in its geology, scenic beauties and remoteness. In his annual reports he mentioned that most visitors valued these features, seeking a retreat from the clamor and artificial constructs of the urban areas. This factor influenced the educational and interpretive work of park rangers, an influence that has endured over the years. He and the first rangers assigned to educational tasks emphasized the natural, ecological aspects of park experience over purely "fun" things. As qualified personnel were engaged, organized educational programs were presented to the public. In August, 1929, Park Naturalist Russell Farmer delivered nature talks to 1,441 visitors and recorded 3,439 individuals visting the Museum. These two figures accounted for 43% of all park visitations that month.

On the recreational front, in the early 'thirties ski enthusiasts pleaded for opportunities to conduct ski events and some family skiing within the Park. After NPS consultations, Collins organized a ski competition in 1934. This was the beginning of a long and sometimes stressful experience with the winter sports public who came primarily from the Northern Sacramento Valley towns (Chico, Red Bluff, and Redding), but also to some extent from Sacramento and the Bay Area. This mounting pressure fundamentally contradicted the early NPS philosophy of park use primarily for its intrinsic, natural qualities. Could winter enjoyment be conducted without the "invasion" of thousands of skiers who, for downhill fun, would require heavy equipment and facilities for tow apparatus, warming houses and first-aid services? This question runs through the entire history of the Park. It requires a qualified answer, for the educational mission of the Park is left hanging in air without closure on the issue.

Hunting and fishing presented a different picture. Due to the decimation and, for some animal species extermination (Grizzly Bear, Wolf, Wolverine, Antelope, Mountain Goat), NPS ruled that no hunting be allowed within the Park. For those animals that had disappeared or nearly so, this policy posed no problem. But for other animals, such as deer which ranged well beyond park boundaries between seasons, it was problematical. Without their natural predators deer herds would grow and impact negatively on available resources within the Park. If suffecient kills were made outside its boundaries, the problem could perhaps be solved. But in the early years park management did not have the knowledge, methods or resources to conduct any kind of rational, coherent recreational policy in behalf of the hunters. Restrictions imposed were quite arbitrary.

For the fishing public, park policy early established a fish planting program that would help restore trout streams from radical decline in the late 1800s. The reckless catches perpetrated by over-greedy settlers and adventurers, who took hundreds of fish at a time way beyond their consumptive needs, had devastating affects on the area's fishing. From the mid-twenties, systematic stocking occurred each year. Streams and lakes were by-and-large opened to the public, with a few exceptions, such as Lake Helen and Emerald Lake near Lassen Peak, two dazzling alpine lakes at high altitudes which were stocked only for tourists' esthetic enjoyment, not for the anglers.

In respect to both hunting and fishing, there was no visible effort during the early years to conduct information programs using scientific knowledge based on natural and ecological data, in order to educate sports-people about those vital aspects of their recreational pursuits. For this category of public user, educational and informational programs based on scientific knowledge would come at a later time.

A similar situation existed with the park flora. As a simple fact of life, Superintendent Collins lacked the resources (personnel and equipment) and the time to lay the foundations necessary for a wholesome and forward-looking set of educational programs in these areas. But he was well aware of their importance. In 1929 he requested NPS assistance for personnel and funds to begin the scientific work needed to support a sound educational program. Except for the appointment of a summer park naturalist in 1929, and again in 1931, he received no direct help. These denials came notwithstanding Albright's success during 1929-1932, in getting budget increases during the Hoover depression years. Overworked during the high tourist months, Collins' small staff could not possibly give due attention to scientific data-gathering and to planning of programs, assuming they were competent to do so. So, notwithstanding Washington's official "encouragement," Lassen Park was unable to move in the desired directions.

There was one exception to this stifling situation: geological research and publication. From 1926, The University of California posted two well qualified geologists to conduct research and reporting work. Drs. R. H. Finch and H. M. Williams spent months each year conducting basic research to elucidate the geological history and volcanic characteristics of the Lassen area. If in any scientific respect the Park merited serious investigation, it would be at least in these two related areas. Without verified information, park personnel could hardly speak with authority about Lassen's most significant feature, its volcanism. In 1932 Dr. Williams published the first definitive though not exhaustive report on the geology of Mt. Lassen and vicinity. This report would be used for future planning of both park development and educational programs. These eminent geologists hosted scientists and researchers from institutions across the country and also from New Zealand, Indonesia, and Switzerland, where geological history similar to that of Lassen created an interest in the Fire Mountain.

Collectively, these conditions, NPS policies, ideas and initiatives at park level, and limited financial provisions for Lassen Park constituted the "foundations of education" up to the appointment, in 1932, of Lassen's first permanent park naturalist. By that time certain "givens" in terms of public expectations about using the Park had already set in. They were in two ideological camps: the true nature lovers who sought both an esthetic experience in and introspective relationship with primitive nature with all its untouched beauties; and the real activists who anticipated having fun and diversion in the Park through its many recreational potentials, especially winter sports. Unlike Yosemite Park's tourists, who had already lobbied for a host of comforts (symbolized by the plush Ahwahnee Hotel), Lassen Park's supporters looked askance at such influences and strove to avoid them.

A special note is due on education outside the park. Mainly because of his personal knowledge of neighboring Valley communities, Walker Collins initiated, pretty much on his own, an outreach program of education in a number of towns. Working through chambers of commerce, he installed small exhibits in store-front windows. He gave talks to service clubs and public agencies. Evening sessions for adults and families, which he called the "School of Lassen," presented photographs and many geological details. He encouraged his over-worked rangers, especially after 1929 when he was granted his first permanent staff, to participate in these outreach programs in the off-season. As there is no precise documentation on the numbers of citizens reached by these means, we can say little about their impacts. Judging from the steadily rising numbers of visitors, campers, and museum attendees, we assume that outreach had some affects.

Through press releases, mimeographed flyers, special events announcements and networking with friends in the valley, Collins and his small staff disseminated lots of information to the general public. The thirst for this information and its affects are seen in the rapid rise in annual numbers of visitors between 1925 and 1931: from 10,000 to almost 60,000 in six years. Then, with the opening of the Loop Road, access to the entire Park attracted steadily increasing numbers. Educational services by qualified naturalists became essential to the Park's mission.

The Development and Fate of Education Programs
In March, 1932, NPS approved the appointment of Norman W. Scherer as Lassen's first Park Naturalist on a permanent basis. Scherer held a Master of Science degree from The University of Michigan, renowned for its strong pro-

grams in the technical and life sciences. He transferred from a similar post at Yellowstone National Park, the oldest and most prestigious among the growing number of national parks. Director Albright had worked hard to make Yellowstone a model of natural conservation and education. At the time, the "interpretation program" at park level was known as the education department (like its Washington counterpart), until 1940.

At regional level, prior to the creation of NPS Regional Offices, Scherer reported to the "Park Naturalist and Forester of the Field Educational and Forestry Headquarters," at The University of California in Berkeley. Ansel F. Hall, a well qualified natural scientist, held this position. He had done pioneering work at Yosemite in both interpretation and museum development. Reports from Scherer in the field were routed to Hall, thence forwarded to Washington.

Collins immediately directed Scherer to produce material for public dissemination, since the Park's stock of hand-out literature consisted of only four small booklets. The new Park Naturalist composed the first of a proposed series entitled, "Ranger Notes" (later renamed "Nature Notes"), covering information on programs for visitors and scientific notes about Lassen's geology and natural resources. Scherer also embarked on an ambitious project to strengthen and expand his public education, or "interpretation," programs. But a series of incidents, which can be traced to NPS-Washington, occurred which stymied his efforts and raised once more the fundamental question of Washington's genuine intent about establishing a firm, scientific foundation for educational and other park management systems. It also raised the spectre of politics.

The first was a directive from NPS Assistant Director H.C. Bryant, dated April 25, 1932. Bryant had been recruited by Albright; both were Californians. It called for careful attention by park naturalists to "head counting" of visitors and their activities in the parks. Of the nine items Bryant requested naturalists to report on, only two had any relationship at all to scientific knowledge. One was museum work, and the other consultations with other professional persons (presumably having scientific significance). This administrative top-on-down decree focused primarily on counting the users of park resources and the contacts made by park personnel. These kinds of data were of particular interest to politicians and budget directors. From Washington's vantage point, the number of people coming through the park and their various contacts, explained the importance or "success" of a particular national park. This political orientation did little to inspire park personnel to produce more fundamental and vital information having relevance to the conditions of a park's ecological components and educational development. NPS Director Albright had to pay close attention to these matters for budgetary reasons, well aware as he was of the intense political rivalries in Congress and the Adminstration over allocations to regional constituencies.

Another incident, which might appear insignificant on the surface, had to do with a paper shortage. Scherer's new public information bulletin, "Ranger Notes," was labeled by NPS as a waste of resources. Although Director Albright had encouraged Collins to get on with his educational plans, his subordinates in Washington ordered Scherer to halt his publication because it consumed "too much mimeograph paper," which cost money! Bryant discussed this "crisis" in memoranda to Scherer on April 29 and May 11, 1932. Mr. Scherer obeyed the order, which came over Superintendent Collins' head, who had not been consulted in the matter. Although he as the superintendent was appointed to operate the Park and by statute was empowered to manage his own domain, his superior baron in Washington intervened to take away his mimeograph paper! Quite a swipe for education, with the baron riding herd and the vassal "eating crow."

A third minor crisis erupted when the Washington office took Lassen's Park Naturalist to task over his periodical reporting work. After arriving at Park Headquarters in Mineral on April 17, 1932, Scherer wrote up each monthly report as required. His regional superior at Berkeley, Ansel Hall, received the reports first, and then sent them off to Washington. The routine had already been established. In October, Hall commended Scherer for his "tabulated analyses ... [which] ... we found ... especially interesting," and thanked him for his "prompt compliance with our ... request." (Memorandum from Hall in October, 1932.) I have personally inspected those monthly reports filed by Scherer and can agree with Halls' assessment of the quality of Scherer's work.

But Mr. Bryant was not satisfied. In 1933 he again wrote to Collins complaining of his Park Naturalist, a letter which was prelude to a major decision affecting Lassen. Exasperated, the seasoned Superintendent with eleven plus years at the helm, bluntly threw the ball back into NPS's lap. In his memorandum, Collins told Bryant (and presumably Albright):

> I am at a loss to know what more can be said about the work here. You have been receiving the complete report of all activities carried on here.... I have just received the July copies of the Superintendent Monthly Reports. I ... found that we were giving as complete, or more complete, information on this branch of our activities than other parks. I thought this was rather good

considering that only one ranger- naturalist has been carrying on this work ...
as compared with the far greater number at Yellowstone and other parks. ...
More space is given to the educational work ... than to any one phase of our
activities."

Bryant admitted that there was "improvement" in Lassen's monthly reporting, but he nonetheless ended Scherer's Lassen career by the time he got around to replying to Collins. Not only was Scherer bounced out of the Park, but also Bryant did not reopen his position until two years later. Collins thus got both a rebuff from the political barony and a freeze on his key staff position. In view of Horace Albright's previous commendations of Walker Collins' performance and achievements, this series of events appears bizarre. At the least, it reflects a kind of political intrigue or perhaps double-dealing that characterizes political systems that are subject to a variety of pressure groups and influence bargainers. While some political careers may well have profited from these dealings, in the end it was the Park and its personnel who suffered the consequences.

This scenario demonstrates clearly that political factors, having little or nothing to do with the reality of managing a national park, at least one park called Lassen, can arbitrarily intervene in the legitimate domain of a park superintendent, who holds his appointment from the Interior Secretary, acting for the President. Whether one calls this behavior "expediency" or "intrigue" or simply "meddling," it reinforced a pattern running throughout the entire history of Lassen Volcanic National Park. I will focus on this theme in another chapter dealing with political expediency, but the reader can also refer to episodes in other chapters that reflect the same pattern. In social science jargon we call this behavior "organizational goal-displacement," or in less genteel terms, "political corruption." A member of the Yana-Yahi tribe would remind us, "Why are you dismayed at white man's treachery?" In a more pointed sense, it appears that the administrative integrity of the superintendent's statutory role was directly undermined by these superordinate moves by the "good old boys," whose portfolios included no direct field responsibilities. Walker Collins tried to build management systems based on good information, not on political considerations.

Collins personally gave attention to establishing a park library, adding accessions from time to time and charging temporary (seasonal) rangers to look after the collection. He also contracted with a private cartographer and relief-map maker, R. C. Lind of San Francisco, to produce such a map for Lassen. When he informed Washington of his plan, he was rebuffed and told by Bryant to work through the appropriate NPS office in San Francisco charged with such model-building. By the time memoranda circulated on the matter, Lind had already completed the work, submitting it to Regional Naturalist Ansel Hall at Berkeley for his inspection. Hall reported that Lind's work was "a superb model and, ... it is practically impossible for us to turn out a finished job which would have all the details as meticulously done ...." One needs again to ask, on what real authority and credibility should NPS interfere in a matter of this kind? It was apparent that, in dealing with his Park's needs, Collins possessed superior judgment to that of someone sitting some three thousand miles away. If it had been a matter of major expenditure, perhaps a second opinion, even from Washington, could have merit. Bryant's behavior has to be labeled as petty, bureaucratic meddling in the superintendent's business.

Without a permanent park naturalist, the educational program could not move forward. Yet, visitors continued to come. In the park report for 1934, nearly 36,000 visitor educational contacts were made, over half of which occurred at the Loomis Museum. This statistic bears out the continuing interest by the public in the history, geology, and natural features of Lassen Park. Collins' community outreach programs also got renewed attention, with rangers going into both the Sacramento and the San Joaquin Valleys to give talks during the slack times in the Park (before July 4th, and from early September). Frequently the local chambers of commerce hosted these events, providing a good network into many community organizations.

With the appointment of Dr. Carl R. Swartzlow in October, 1935, to the park naturalist post, Lassen's educational prospects brightened. A geologist holding a doctorate from The University of Missouri, Swartzlow brought a high level of scientific attention to the Park's educational and interpretive mission. Pursuing work laid down by Professor Howell Williams from University of California-Berkeley, he undertook as time allowed studies of volcanism and also gave a lot of attention to reequipping the Museum with more genuine, scientifically significant specimens. Theretofore, its main focus was the photographic collections of Benjamin Loomis, but it also included questionable artifacts, placed there at random without benefit of scientific scrutiny. Their authenticity and value could be challenged. Swartzlow paid less attention to monthly reports on visitor activities, but this shift in priorities did not seem to raise eyebrows in Washington. This change in bureaucratic demeanor seems to be related to the ouster of Lynne Walker Collins in July, 1935, previously mentioned.

Dr. Swartzlow introduced for the first time a Native American component to the education program in 1936 (See Figure 1-3.) Descendants of the Atsugewi people engaged in basket weaving, displays of native costumes and methods of food preparation. Except for a few lapses for certain years, this cultural and historical theme became a permanent part of the Lassen heritage in park interpretation programs. He also gave immediate attention to audiovisual resources, adding considerable equipment and urging the superintendent to make campgrounds more amenable to talks and demonstrations. His most insistent request was for a bona-fide visitors center, where both naturalist presentations and films could be shown. The Museum "auditorium," in the rear of the building, was a cramped place with few technical amenities to accomodate competent professionals and their media needs. The building was also damp and uncomfortable, with poor lighting and air circulation. The exhibit cases in the main part of the structure were primitive, poorly lighted and not given to displaying artifacts.

As with previous requests during the Collins years, Dr. Swartzlow's fell on unsympathetic ears. Washington bureaucrats always seemed to have a valid excuse, such as "low priority" for such rudimentary things as visitors centers. Without this building, a truly professional job of presenting Lassen's unusually attractive features to the public, as the 1929 NPS education report had urged, remained a foggy and distant vision. Swartzlow's repeated requests went unheeded by NPS-Washington.

Two primary factors underlay any national park's capacity to deliver on its educational mission: Qualified personnel, and adequate facilities for personnel to work in. Lassen had the personnel, but was starved for facilities. Swartzlow performed in high fashion, making contacts with many national and international geologists concerned with volcanism, many of whom visited the Park to consult with him. Botanists came from a variety of research and teaching centers. He also delivered a number of scientific papers at geological symposia around the country. And he managed to have a new seismograph from The University of California installed in 1938. It is a sad comment that he had such little support from the NPS hierarachy. Had he enjoyed an open forum where he could fairly present his agenda in comparison with those of other park naturalists, the story might well have been quite different. But decision-making in NPS did not operate in an open forum where all relevant participants shared equal time.

Dr. Swartzlow required the rangers at various ranger stations across the Park, to report as best they could on natural and scientific matters coming to their attention. This information increased the knowledge base of the Park as a whole, and enabled those engaged in program development to work with more reliable information for planning. One Chief Park Ranger, Eugene Barton, cooperated to the point of making lists of wildlife classified by Latin nomenclatures. One of the seasonal rangers, Julian Vogt, compiled lists of birds and plants, based on part-time obeservations. No one was appointed the important task of such inventorying on a permanent basis. The Park simply did not have the means or policy-directives for building a knowledge base of scientific information.

Park Naturalist Swartzlow's efforts nonetheless raised the level of educational and scientific efforts at Lassen. While it is very difficult to compare them to other parks' conduct of education, it seems clear that Swartzlow set as high a standard as possible under limiting circumstances. This standard set a permanent benchmark for future Lassen naturalists-interpreters. But it would be many years, not until the late 1950's, before Lassen Park would have any opportunity for a further upgrading of its educational programs.

Educational Development in the Post-Mission 66 Period

The post-World War II years at Lassen, as with all the national parks, focused primarily on renewal of physical plants and infrastructures. The famous Mission 66 policy begun in 1956 responded to the poor conditions in those areas, primarily employee housing. As we've already seen, however, Lassen Park benefitted little from that Federal-level thrust. The Park's continuing number-one priority, a visitors center, failed again to gain recognition at NPS Regional and Federal levels. Nonetheless, park naturalists at Lassen labored on and made new contributions to visitor education. A few of their accomplishments merit special commendation among the some 25-30 specific areas of responsibility that a typical, full-time park naturalist was supposed to cover.

Around 1950, 60% of the park naturalist's responsibilities related to educational and scientific work, while 40% had to do with administrative and routine work. In trying to implement their professional duties, however, park staff labored under a major disadvantage. During the period from 1946 to about 1960, NPS did not encourage recruitment of sufficient park naturalists trained in a scientific discipline to replenish their ranks decimated since the War. Its policy emphasized the expediency of transfering rangers from protection service over to duties of interpretation. At Lassen, Superintendet Fred Johnson was seeking to strengthen his interpretation staff with an assistant naturalist. He was instructed by his superior at the San Francisco Regional Office that it was a good thing that the park naturalist position be filled by a generalist, rather than by a specialist, because specialization may not serve the public as well as would a broad viewpoint. In a memorandum dispatched in May, 1952, the NPS Regional Naturalist,

D. G. Yeager, informed him that the regular, old protection-type ranger's "participation [in] other departments is becoming more and more common in national parks. It is an excellent idea and exemplifies something of which we are all aware, ... that all park personnel have the same objective, that is, service to the public."

While this sentiment derived from a sense of dedication to the public interest at large, it negated a long-held policy commitment of NPS to nurture a scientific and highly professional approach to interpretation and to program planning. To the extent that Ranger Yeager's viewpoint became a widely accepted norm for recruiting park naturalists, the door opened to assigning many "generalists" to positions requiring considerably greater knowledge and skills than those individuals typically had. Such a personnel policy would not only "water down" the quality of education and scientific information services, but also affect career development and the overall quality of leadership throughout NPS.

A typical program for the public covered museum visits, hiking on trails marked with self-instructional guides, geological history, nature and wildlife talks, and Native American culture (See Figure 5-1.) A main concession that NPS made to Lassen Park was the construction of a 300-seat amphitheatre at Manzanita Lake Campgrounds for outdoor programming. While the facility did not in any way substitute as a permanent structure for information, sales, exhibits and audio-visual programs, it served thousands of interested visitors each season. By the 1960's, all of Lassen's interpretation programs reached several hundred thousand individuals a year.

While many park naturalists at Lassen have served with distinction, one individual stands out as superb in terms of his dedicated work on education and scientific reporting. The fact that Park Naturalist Paul E. Schultz (1947-1955) served during a time of NPS back-sliding in terms of qualifications for appointment to this position, makes his contributions all the more noteworthy. He served in his post without an assistant, apparently due to Superintendent Johnson's request for a specialist having been denied by NPS. Nonetheless, Park Naturalist Schultz worked prodigiously at program innovation. He researched both the natural history of the Park and its cultural forbearers, the Native Americans. These efforts produced two very popular books sold through the Loomis Museum Association retail program.

Schultz's first book dealt with the "rocks of Lassen" and was entitled, *Geology of Lassen's Landscapes*, 1952. It was completed five years after his appointment to Lassen Volcanic, and filled a very real need for a readable and well illustrated booklet on the geological orgins and formations of the Park. A unique feature of the book is its explanation of geological characteristics around each major volcanic phenomenon, as well as some non-volcanic ones, where park interpretation aids were located. Thus, at "Bumpass Hell," the known origins of these boiling springs, or hydro-thermal hotbeds, are described in considerable detail in language that the lay visitor can grasp. It has enjoyed a along and profitable life among the Park's publications.

His second work, first published in 1954, *Indians of Lassen*, was a scholarly book produced not by an ethnologist but by a scientifically trained naturalist. His reliance on ethnographic and anthropological sources compensated for his lack of original training in those fields. Covering most of the published literature on the tribal peoples who once inhabited Lassen Country, it provides an excellent account of the origins, development, cultural ways and life styles of the four predominant tribes of the region. Revised and updated by the documented history of Ishi, Schultz's book was republished in 1988. It is the only work of its kind on the "park Indians" of California and remains a popular item for visitors. Few park naturalists have equalled or excelled Paul Schultz in scientific contributions to a national park.

With the publication in 1959 of a revised NPS Manual, park interpretation work was encouraged to adopt a more scientific orientation, so as to build a higher quality service in both education and overall management. A new educational policy had been set. The role of park naturalist was sharpened to focus on the intrinsic values and resources of the park so as to heighten visitors' awareness and appreciation of natural and cultural features. This re-emphasis of fundamentals anticipated a period of nation-wide development of environmental, ecological and preservationist ethics in America. These values implied emphasis on restoration, primitive nature, use of scientific knowledge and the like, as against programs aimed primarily at pleasing and entertaining the user public, along lines advocated by Ranger Yeager. Education then would be the primary means for generating visitor concern for preservation and unimpairment, while law enforcement, or "protection," would take a lesser role in overall park policy and management, notwithstanding Ranger Yeager's preferences for the good old generalist armed with a "trusty .38", that is, the protection and law enforcement ranger.

Lassen's staff responded positively to these themes, in keeping with the Park's long history favoring the primitive experience. Their 1963 Master Plan called for interpretive programs that offered visitors a "full appreciation of ... geological processes ... while still affording protection to this priceless heritage." It recommended a mature research program to create the needed data base for studies and programs about the geology, wild life and fauna in the Park. Both a visitors center and a standard, well stocked library were also requested. This master plan document did not, however, receive official approval at the Regional Office, and it remained on the shelf until 1966, when a revised plan was pulled together. Apparently Ranger Yeager and friends had not yet gotten the message. Due to lack of NPS support, the new document actually down-played the role of interpretation! Interpretive staff did not have the physical resources to display their "wares" anyway. But the need for a visitors center again figured in the hope-for expansion of interpretation, which NPS policy was stressing during the sixties. This focus was reflected in Lassen's educational programs in 1967, whose themes were:

- Predators and prey, wildlife checks and balances
- Nature, the master weaver, natural environment complexes
- Beyond the forest edge, discovering nature
- The web of life; interrelationships of living things to one another and their environment
- The big picture, makeup of the Park's natural environment
- Wilderness — friend or foe, invitation to the backcountry
- Wildlife habitats and habitants
- Landscape by fire; formation of Lassen's landscape
- Lassen's waters; importance of water in a natural area

All these programs delivered information and concepts of scientific character, rather than entertainment or amusement. Regularly scheduled wilderness hikes, guided by qualified and experienced naturalists knowledgeable about Lassen Country, reinforced these subjects. Brochures for each wilderness area provided detailed information on what to expect and how to interpret observations. A primary source for wilderness hiking was a booklet, "Lassen Trails" (1963), prepared by an experienced backcountry ranger, Steve Matteson. With thirty-four trails featured, this source enabled the true nature lover to commune with any chosen aspect of the park. Twenty years later, this booklet was supplemented by a still more elaborate one, "Hiking Trails of Lassen Volcanic National Park," by George Perkins (1983).

Reflecting even more the growing movement toward public environmental responsibilities was an educational manual for teachers and learners: "Lily Pond

Environmental Study Area: Teacher Handbook (A reference book to aid in developing environmental awareness)." This neat little volume presented an holistic view of biotic communities inhabiting a small water ecosystem a short distance from Reflection Lake at the northwest corner of the Park. An exquisite spot hidden in the woods, this pond lent itself well to small groups of children and adults intent on acquiring a first-hand knowledge of nature's complex and fascinating life cycles. (Figure 5-1.) The teaching manual addressed four objectives: *first*, to present the cultural and natural environment to the learner, of which the human is a part; *second*, to generate in the learner an understanding of how humans both use and misuse natural resources; *third*, to offer opportunities for learners to work directly with problem-solving methods; and *fourth*, to enable learners to become responsible members of the park community.

This fascinating educational project expressed the highest point in environmental education and awareness that the Park's interpretation program had attained up to that time. And it was made easily accesible to any interested and motivated park visitor. Park records have not recorded the number of occasions the program was used, or how many visitors, including school excursions to the Park, actually experienced it. The question of available, qualified staff to operate this type of field education was, however, raised during the mid-sixties by Lassen's chief park naturalist. He estimated that, to do justice to all the educational programs at his command and perform professionally, he would need a minimum of 640 man-hours of work per week, during the peak season months. That translated into sixteen employees (excluding administrative support personnel) working a 40-hour week. His available staff numbered significantly less than that requirement.

Meanwhile, the visitors continued to rise to the point that around 1970 over one-half million people entered each year. In 1972 the number approached 600,000. Given its size and the number of park service personnel, Lassen was accomodating more people than either Yosemite or Yellowstone (whose equivalent figures would have to be multiplied at least seven and twenty times, respectively, based on park size.) Lassen's work force was certainly "carrying its load" while performing a high quality educational program under conditions that neither Yosemite or Yellowstone had ever encountered. Yet, official records on Lassen's deprived situation reflect the opinion by bureaucrats that the Park's management did not merit any higher level of support. On the assumption that NPS leaders truly cared about this Park, they did not seem to understand arithmetic nor how to evaluate park staff performance.

In 1976 Lassen's staff cranked out a new "General Management Plan," a comprehensive planning document that replaced the old "master plan" format. This document advanced even further the concepts of wilderness preservation and visitor appreciation of both the natural and cultural heritages. The provisions for human "use and entertainment" were considerbly scaled back, although a place for "family skiing" continued to surface. This GMP stated that the Park's main mission was, "to restore the terrestrial and aquatic ecosystems ... that most probably existed prior to technological disturbances by man." This statement was the boldest one yet coming from the staff planning efforts since the 1929 pronouncements about the central educational purpose of Lassen Park, in regard to natural preservation.

The only element left out, but a most significant one, was restoration of aboriginal cultures. Such a plan would have seemed ludicrous in view of historical reality. But one needs to remember that a major segment of Lassen Country's heritage remained forever absent from that reality. An acknowledgement of that fact came with one of the plan's objectives, to explore "historic and archeological resources in the park" and to secure their protection.

These points called for even more attention to and training by park naturalists in ecologically related disciplines and methods of educational presentation. The plan called for coverage of all "biotic features ... focusing on how life adapts to changeable volcanic landscapes ...."

The new mission focus seemed threatened, however, by a catastrophic policy decision imposed on Lassen Park in 1974: closure of the popular and comparatively well-situated visitor facilities at Manzanita Lake, the Park's "jewel" site for receiving visitors (I will deal with this event in Chapter 6.) What the park naturalist staff had to work with, both before and after closure, was a puny A-frame building plopped down at the side of the entrance road by the U.S. Forest Service. The structure was an insult to the grandeur, tradition, and personnel of one of America's most impressive and interesting national parks. It is not too strong to label NPS's response to Lassen's needs as a "disgrace to the nation," as well as to Northern California communities.

Notwithstanding this deplorable situation, five years after the Manzanita Lake closure park staff processed 507,807 visitors through their educational and recreational services. They earned the commendation of all, but received little real reward from NPS officials who continued still to deny them the conditions which their professional roles required.

One of the more recent Chief Park Naturalists, Richard Vance (retired, 1991), persevered for twenty years under this blight of neglect. A few years prior to his termination, Dick Vance put in plans for films, audio-visual equipment, including way-side solar powered units, and a goodly number of other needed interpretive modules. Although the total price tag came under a quarter of a million dollars, NPS's slow, foot-dragging responses to these proposals produced only a partial completion of the "wish list" by the time Vance retired. What more can be said about NPS leadership since the days of Norman Scherer and Carl Swartzlow?

Yet another, "final" planning document came out in 1981: "General Management Plan," supplanting that of 1976. One of its highlights was a focus on the Park's cultural resources: Native American artifacts which had been donated or else discovered by both archeologists and amateur collectors; emigrant trails; pioneer relics; early structures built by settlers, government agents (Forest Service, Park Service, etc.), or commercial enterprises; and the like. Ever since Lassen Peak and Cinder Cone had become national monuments in 1907, the Government had concern for preserving the records of cultural development. Until the Loomis Museum was created in 1927 there had been little space for storing collectibles. And until a definite policy emerged, and the means to implement it, the Park could not effectively manage cultural resources.

While the Museum had always been a popular tourist attraction, due in good part to Ben Loomis' fabulous photographs of the volcanic eruptions during 1914 - 1921, he and his family and friends collected many specimens that were improperly identified or labeled. Geological and natural specimens were also unevenly representative of the Park, or inappropriately classified. Park Naturalist Swartzlow had repeatedly sought funds to revamp the Museum and to transfer many perishable items to a new visitor center. He designed three main collection departments: Geological History, History of Lassen Peak, and Plant and Animal Life. He recommended structural changes and a revised layout plan. Almost fifty years later, his recommendations were still in the state they were in when he made them: recommendations.

Dr. Swartzlow had also founded in 1939 the "Loomis Museum Association," a for-profit enterprise for collecting information about the Park and publishing it in brochures, pamphlets and books for sale to the general public. His plans for the Association included a library, audio-visual instructional facilities, and program activities beneficial to the Park. Over the ensuing years, this Association has contributed enormously to the Park's success and to helping to enlarge, through wise use of its income, the range of park services.

Later efforts to follow through on Swartzlow's plans and dreams met with little success at Regional and National Offices. In 1958 a new "Museum Prospectus and Development Outline" was submitted for budgetary consideration, and again in the early sixties. Each time the proposals were returned without recommendation for funding. Over the years park naturalists used odd rooms and closets located around the headquarters area to house valuable specimens, such as herbs and other flora, which could not be kept at the Museum due to humidity. Plans for a full museum restoration were eventually shelved, in anticipation that a real visitors center would render that step unnecessary. In the end, neither venture ever took place until 1993, when $40,000 were generated by private contributions to refurbish the museum. This amount of money, however, was a mere dribble of what the Park truly needs and ranked far below outlays for visitor facilities in other parks.

Even as late as 1981, therefore, park planners realized that their cultural program still lacked coherence, consistency and a scientific approach. Aboriginal dwelling places had been documented in different ways, using unorthodox nomenclatures and non-uniform descriptive styles. Cartographic methods varied and lacked consistent terminology. A complete and verified list of historic buildings within park boundaries had not been compiled after seventy years of park existence. The photograpahic collections, especially colored slides, needed to be reclassified and numbered. It appeared to the Park's managers that the entire cultural program area was in desperate need of basic work and general upgrading by professionally qualified staff. Monies had to be allocated to begin the process, and also the spectre of Chaos Crags hanging over the Manzanita Lake visitor site would have to be dealt with before any major transformation of the Museum could occur, and before an appropriate facility for a complete cultural education program could be created.

Whether NPS officials and their congressional allies will, in the future, provide the financial resources and leadership for cultural redevelopment at Lassen, remains still a major question. Perhaps the very least we could expect, in the absence of some major private donation, is money to rehabilitate fully the physical structure of the museum. Such a step would only be a minor one, however, in the face of the huge needs that Lassen Park has accumulated over the past half century. (See Notes.)

If indeed the educational mission of a grand park such as Lassen Volcanic still remains its highest priority, then we should expect much more attention and consideration by NPS leadership. In spite of major financial shortcomings, the park naturalists at Lassen over the decades have performed outstanding work, which has been recognized more than once in awards bestowed on the Park's Interpreter Division. One of its small but very valuable accomplishments has been the establishment of a register of historical structures in the Park.

The next chapter examines the record of management in regard to the park's restorative mission and the approach taken at Lassen Volcanic to fulfill its assigned mission. What kinds of political expediency arose over the years to confront park staff?

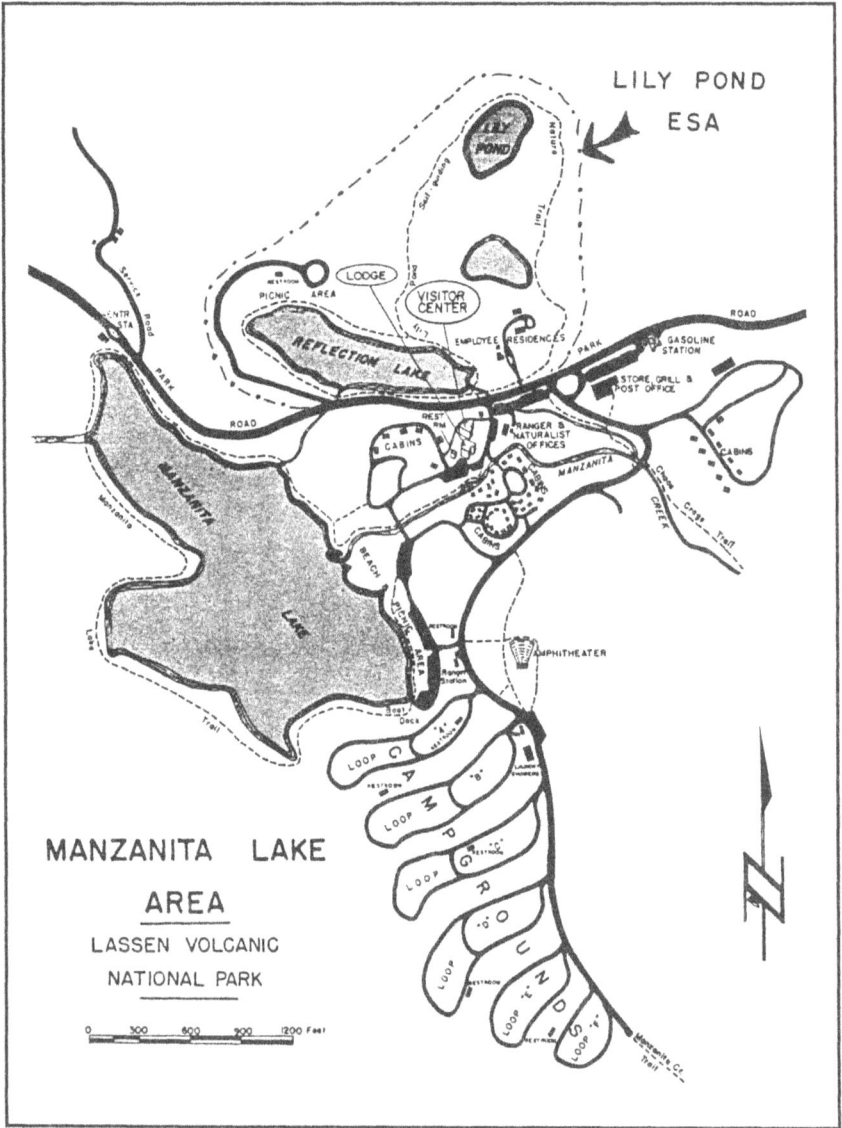

LILY POND
ESA

MANZANITA LAKE
AREA

LASSEN VOLCANIC
NATIONAL PARK

0   300   600   900   1200 Feet

5-1. Lily Pond Envirnmental Study Area

CHAPTER 6

MANAGING PARK RESOURCES: POLICY SCIENCE
VS. POLITICAL EXPEDIENCY
(or "Going by the seat of the pants")

Backgrounds to the Issues

If ever in modern history Americans had an open door, a convenient path toward changing our behavior and relationships with the natural world, the national parks movement affords that opportunity. The parks were created to help reeducate citizens in the arts of natural living and in genuine appreciation of earth's primeval conditions. They offer the nation an alternative to the urban environment, to the isolated suburb and inner city, to dependence on mechanization of all modes of living. Can national parks be managed so as to afford these choices? Will they be preserved as genuine schools of wilderness? The answers to these questions lie in the soundness of national parks policy, the quality of park management, in the effectiveness of reeducation and in the enlightenment of park users.

We in America took the first feeble step in these directions with the creation of Yellowstone National Park in 1872 and, a few years later, of Yosemite. Early naturalists like John Muir and Aldo Starker Leopold promoted a preservation movement that supported creating national parks across the nation. As previously discussed, the issues of how best to determine policies and manage these preserves arose when problems of their users' values, habits, and preferences faced park managers with wrenching dilemmas and frequent hard choices.

The legislative and presidential acts establishing parks did not specify or delineate the kinds of activities to be permitted or forbidden. These specifications would come only with time and experience. But the basic laws and administrative directives governing the parks did imply that management impose a regimen that secured the ethic and promoted the goals of "natural unimpairment."

In the view of one dedicated observer and student of our park system, Freeman Tilden, our national parks reflect a "scheme of land use so far removed from the average person's economic experience" that it appears "strange and remote." "The national parks are not merely places of spectacular scenic features ... . [and] not merely places of physical recreation." These preserves "would justify their existence even if they did not possess so great a scenic merit." National parks exist in order to preserve for posterity, in the words of the 1916 Act, "the scenery and the natural and historic objects and the wild life" within their boundaries. They exist "to ensure that the process of nature can work, without artifice...," and "to keep intact in the wilderness areas all the historic and prehistoric evidences of occupation by our predecessors." These are the objects of managing a park's natural and cultural resources, including our Native American heritage.

Not all Americans have accepted these definitions of purpose, which emerged from the experiences and heart-felt values of those who struggled for about a half century to create, under law, our national park system. There are even deeper philosophical differences about the real nature of this earth and universe, its finite or infinite qualities, limited or unlimited resources, that create differing views about how to deal with their use and or conservation in national preserves. Such dissent from Federal statute and park rules explains why issues have arisen about how human management should perform its function of preserving the world's most magnificent national park domains. Legal provisions and their interpretations by National Park Service officials, as well as by millions of park lovers and users, have required that systems be created to implement the laws, regulations, and decisions that enable the parks to function and perpetuate their existence.

This process has included many protectionist measures to prevent disturbance and spoliation of resources, and have initiated, from time to time, efforts at establishing some measurable base lines or scientific criteria which would tell park managers whether or not their efforts actually preserved park resources. Such measures would also seem to include collecting scientific data about the state of "wilderness," particularly during those years when wilderness legislation took effect in the national parks. Measurement based on concrete data also implies specific evaluation methods which tell managers "where things are" at any given point in time.

Just how to go about exercising such controls, and what kinds of management techniques, in terms of human behaviors, organization, and physical-technical arrangements, are subjects that NPS officials, park managers, and employees have discussed for decades. They constitute the crux of this phase of our story, and Lassen Volcanic National Park offers us a convenient locale and experience for "testing out" the efficacy of different approaches to preserving the natural and cultural resources of a national park. As already defined, Lassen lies in a remote area of northeastern California, and at the time of its creation only a few small towns forty to fifty miles distant represented the advancing urban culture of industrial America. Today, those communities are still somewhat small. But access to the region is greatly facilitated by a network of national and state freeways which bring it within three to eight driving hours from almost any point in California and many neighboring states.

For those members of the public and pressure groups who do not agree with the above concepts about values, goals and management criteria, there is a different way of looking at the national parks. These interests have been and remain very articulate in Northern California communities. They have lobbied very effectively over the years. Briefly put, their position is that the parks are public property, domains of the citizen taxpayer, and as such ought to be freely accessible to them for whatever purpose they so choose. They are there to be "enjoyed!"

The pre-1916 users of Lassen Park did just that: they enjoyed and used every possible aspect of the mountain wilderness, at the expense of the Native American dwellers. Their attitudes are still with us. They want to hunt, fish, play, ride horses, pick wildflowers, cut wood and dig up trees in "their park." These viewpoints have over the years rubbed off on or tainted some NPS administrators and employees. The aggressiveness and sheer numbers of people who have pressured NPS for liberalizing the statutes and regulations governing the Park to allow more "fun" face park managers with difficult decisions.

A few years ago I was hiking in Lassen backcountry when I spotted a 4 X 4 pickup, spotlights and all, parked well off one of the park service roads. A mile or so up the trail I heard dogs barking and wild shouting. On getting closer to the scene, I observed a large German Shepherd, beautiful creature, treeing a gray squirrel. A second hound was chasing another wild animal across an open space in the forest. I asked the young men if they knew that domestic dogs as predators were illegal in the Park. One of the boys replied, "We always come here to run our dogs, and it's none of your d... business!" I asked if they had a wilderness permit issued by the park ranger. "What do we need a permit for? This is our Park. We live near here and we do what we want, OK?"

When reporting the incident back at Park Headquarters, I was informed that there's just too much territory to monitor with a limited staff. All they can do is to control the tourists driving through the entrance stations, camping in the official campgrounds and hiking the established trails. Management faces a lot of tough challenges. Public education, including in-park information systems, may be the only possible answer to the need for more responsible user behaviors. This "other viewpoint" about the goals and purposes of a national park would have management make decisions only by "the seat of the pants," or by "crisis management," on an ad hoc and expedient basis. Or, simply make no decisions at all. This story explores many examples of such "management" as well as the slow development, over many decades, of a policy-science process. (See Notes for references for this chapter.)

Concepts of Resources Management: The Meagre Beginnings

NPS philosophy and the influences of early preservationists provided an ethical framework, if not a methodology, for guiding the organization, procedures and management of Lassen Park. Superintendent Walker Collins and his seasonal aides first tried to secure the physical boundaries of the Park so that loggers and domesticated livestock could not violate it. At length he was obliged to charge cattlemen fees for grazing their stock in the meadows; a first, painful concession to the ranchers' economic pressure group. Timber harvesting was another troublesome aspect, but with the help of the ranchers, whose cattle liked to browse along stream banks often devastated by lumbering operations, Collins was able to terminate lumbering by the timber industry inside the Park. These problems were the more troublesome kind and related only sparingly to the overall need for scientific information to guide sound policy-making for both conservation and preservation.

In line with his own thinking and with the NPS Education Committee's call in 1929 for a scientific information system, Collins began to inventory the wildlife within park boundaries. One such inventory was an "Animal Census" done in 1930. While a limited inventory indeed, it established a benchmark for later observations. The absence of the Grizzly Bear reflected the full-scale slaughtering of that animal even before the turn of the 20th century. An old-timer reported that the last Grizzly was shot in 1890 about ten miles southwest of the village of Mineral.

Thereafter, few records were made of the multitude of biota within the Park. Part of the explanation for this lies in the fact that Collins' request for research funds was denied, as already mentioned. Also Park Naturalist Scherer, who was working on plans for a scientific program at Lassen, was harrassed in his post and eventually dismissed. A two-year vacancy in the position ensued and filled only in late 1935 by Dr. Swartzlow. As a geologist he decided to concentrate his scientific work on volcanism and related knowledge. A few years later, several seasonal park naturalists were compiling inventories of various bird and animal species. Professor J. Grinnel at The University of California was monitoring this kind of work and making recommendations to the Regional Office. But no real science policy was in the making.

Birth of a Policy Science for Resources Management: Prelude to Restoration of Wilderness?

After the impasse created by World War II, there was no sign of interest by NPS in building scientific information systems to monitor what was happening in the Park's ecosystems. It was not until the period of Mission 66 (1956-66) that activity renewed. In fact, the years 1930 - 1955 were the most sterile, science-wise (except in geology) of the entire history of the Park. Excluding geological inquiries, 70% of all scientific studies were done after 1966, that is, during the most recent twenty years of the Park's seventy-year history (1916-1986, the dates used for this analysis). This late productivity coincided with renewed emphasis by the general public, and especially by the conservationist-preservationist associations, on the values of America's natural endowments and her vast wilderness areas in particular. While we really can't identify here a cause-and-effect relationship, it is obvious to the careful observer of natural preservation initiatives and of national park management that the two spheres interacted with each other. It resembled a "soul and body" relationship.

Already with the publication during 1959-60 of the revised NPS Manual for park administration, we see renewed attention to certain themes: identifying measures for recording human impacts on natural and cultural resources; need for research projects to establish a scientific management system; bringing visitor programs in line with a park's total management plan; and other directives calling for park restoration to conditions that would secure natural biotic communities, erase human-caused deterioration, protect rare species, support primitive natural zones and contain the rate of human consumption of park resources. All this meant a reduction in human uses of resources, in the spirit of aboriginal culture.

In the early sixties, the abiding influence of Professor Aldo Starker Leopold of The University of Wisconsin, who had been a life-long student and researcher of primitive nature, rose rapidly in the policy debates. Leopold acquired much of his training and experience in the 'twenties working in New Mexico, the "Land of Enchantment," where vast wilderness zones still lay intact, but in need of protection. The Advisory Committee to the U.S. Secretary of Interior, Stuart Udall, issued the famous "Leopold Report" (Wildlife Management in the National Parks) in March, 1963. Udall ordered all park superintendents to use the document as a guide for revising park policies and management. They must "take charge" of their fiefs. Its recommendations reinforced and deepened NPS's guidelines, mentioned above, advocating that a "national park should represent a vignette of primitive America." This bold imagery envisioned a rolling back of park lands to a state of pre-industrial, even pre-settler conditions, akin to the kind of nature that the Native Americans knew prior to European occupation. Management should recognize and promote the diverse ecological communities in each park; should stress only "native plants and animals," to the exclusion of externally induced or "exotic" species; and establish research programs commensurate with the scientific requirements of holisitic management. In concrete terms it called for policy grounded in scientific knowledge, rather than tradition and "best guess," or "seat-of-my-pants" approaches.

Lassen Park's staff was soon at work on its first "Resources Management Plan," in line with instructions from NPS based on the Leopold Report. This action represented the first truly disciplined effort at creating a scientific basis for park management. Unfortunately, if expectations had been high as to the quality of this plan, they proved to be illusive. It appears that the park staff at Mineral Headquarters did not at the time have the professional skills nor manpower to respond adequately to such expectations. The staffing policies advocated by NPS officials like Regional Ranger Yeager, that "generalists" and not specialists be used for all positions, including park naturalists, had not attracted the kind of personnel adequate for this task.

Park Naturalist Paul Schultz, who retired in 1957, was an exception. For example, NPS policy required that the "primary goal of park management is to maintain the biotic associations within each park as nearly as possible in that relationship which existed at a predetermined time period." The optimum time period would be prior to nationalization and introduction of visitors on a large scale. Careful scientific inventorying was essential to such a mission. And it required specific competencies to carry out.

The draft plan called for a research program adequate to all around park management, adherence to land use specifications, elimination of structures adversely affecting natural features, review and regulation of visitor uses detrimental to the environment and other disciplined measures leading to park restoration to a state of "unimpairment." The resources management system would "recognize and respect wilderness as a whole environment of living things whose use and enjoyment depend on a continuing interrelationship free of man's spoliation."

At that time, Lassen Park's knowledge base, its physical capacity to implement the new policies, and professional personnel were inadequate to these objectives. The stock of knowledge in the park library as well as staff access to scientific reports on Lassen's ecology, except for geology and volcanism, simply did not measure up to the tasks outlined. For example, in the section on managing native species, the plan's references to various animals and fowl were incomplete and reflected poorly documented classifications. This kind of "management" was surely going by the seat-of-the-pants! In the final analysis, this fact did not make any real difference, since the proposed Resources Management Plan never received NPS approval beyond the Park's boundaries. This failure of NPS support repeated a well worn pattern. But the fact that park officials did recognize the importance for good management systems of reliable scientific information, was at least a sign of progress.

At the same time, park planners retained winter skiing as a legitimate program, notwithstanding its contradiction with the wilderness concept. It was seen by park management as a "family activity" and therefore relatively harmless and good for public relations. The archeological values of land where ski tow equipment, slope engineering and buildings made their marks had not yet surfaced in park decision-making processes.

Mandate for Scientific Management: Lassen Wilderness

A more scientific and bolder management tool was developed in 1972 for the Park's wilderness zones which were greatly increased by congressional act in October, 1972: 78,982 acres, or almost 80% of the entire Park, fell under the criteria for wilderness management. Park leadership and professional staff now faced greater challenges than ever before to establish scientific decision-making systems for management.

Legislation forbade any human intrusion for economic or physical development that contravened wilderness use. Hiking trails were acceptable, but a souvenir kiosk was definitely taboo! An extremely important provision of the act deleted a portion of a 1930 U.S. Statute that had allowed the Federal Government to authorize mineral explorations within national parks. This disallowance had capital importance for a highly geothermal-active area such as Lassen Park.

117

In a broader sense, it protected the Park from economic exploitation of its natural resources. By further implication, the new law empowered NPS to halt any attempt to intrude in a manner that would threaten the Park's natural integrity, including trespassing its boundaries. Acreage still held by private owners lying inside the Park would therefore be governed by the new provision. Applying the law would be the joint responsibility of the park superintendent and his NPS superiors. One escape clause allowed the Forest Service access roads through sections of the Park to reach its forest lands not otherwise accessible.

Once again, Lassen's professional staff set to work on another resources management plan, this time focusing only on the wilderness zones. In this go-round the NPS Regional Office in San Francisco specified the criteria for guiding the plan. This administrative decision reflected the steadily growing authority exercised by the middle management people at Regional level who did not actually manage any territory or programs per se, but rather "ex officio," under the NPS Director in Washington, inherited authority over the parks. But no federal statute bestowed this power to act in behalf of a park superintendent, who held appointment from the Interior Secretary. It thus became possible for "absentee landlords" to make decisions from their offices hundreds, perhaps thousands, of miles away. The park superintendent had in time become a pawn in the politics of Federal government, having no longer a direct link to the NPS Director, Interior Secretary, or President, from whom he held his authority. A new bureaucracy had grafted itself in between the constitutional lines of authority, an interstice of dubious merit.

One of the most important criteria for plan development was the creation of a central information system at park level containing all relevant data and references on the park's ecosystems. The system should be designed "for defining resource management objectives, ... gaps in knowledge for effective management decisions, ... and implementation of natural resource management programs." Ulitmately such an information center would facilitate creating a basic methodology for ecosystem survey applied to the entire Park. At least conceptually, a policy science for park decision-making, management and systems evaluation had arrived. It was time for the administrators-managers to abandon their traditional and personalized styles. The only remaining question was, did the Lassen park staff have the wherewithal to implement this new theory and method?

In 1973 a "Wilderness Management Study for Lassen Volcanic National Park" was completed and presented as a plan, although the title did not use that term. This document used a new statistical concept called the "ecological unit" for recording all relevant data on the specific resource, its human use or non-use, its operational features within the total park system and other information, as appropriate.

Plans would receive annual operational review at park level as to implementation, and a five-year review through public meetings designed to assess progress. This provision for open public dicussion and citizen participation reflected a practice dating back to the Collins era. Superintendent Collins had been one of the first park managers to "take his case to the public," so-to-speak. He firmly believed that an informed citizenry would be a supportive one, and Walker Collins personally spent much time going into the towns and villages giving talks, listening to people and carrying the Park's message directly to the people who pay the taxes. He urged his rangers to do likewise as schedules permitted.

Under the 1973 plan all wilderness users must make application for backcountry entry, receive educational materials and instructions on regulations and abide by limited time frames governing length of stay. The density of human presence in the wilderness was set so as not to overpopulate the zones at any one time and to limit human impacts. New criteria on wilderness management, and upgraded qualifications for rangers, would require a new park position: Resource Management Specialist. This officer would be primarily responsible for implementing the new plan. Within two years of the plan's completion, Alan Denniston was appointed in 1977. He was faced with a huge operational task of readying all wilderness areas for human use, on a limited scale, and of establishing a new knowledge base for monitoring the conditions of plant and animal life in the wake of wilderness use.

The Lassen Wilderness Plan presented park managers with the first opportunity to create a scientific management system applied to a clearly defined set of use objecitves. It was truly a cut and dried situation. The plan unequivocally stated that management aimed to "preserve the wilderness and to provide for a quality experience for the visitor." A primary challenge to this aim was the fact that the plan allowed hikers to enter the Park at twenty-six different points, all of which could not be monitored by existing staff. Again, the door seemed open to aoat of the pants management, until funding could cover costs of controlling access. Out of ninety-one campsites, fifty-one were designated as "individual," that is one-person camping. Limits were set at twenty hikers on a trail at any one time, and the number of horses at fifteen. The inclusion of the horse reflected a major concession to the equestrian societies, which lobbied hard during the legislative and planning phases. They did enjoy a friendly advocate at both the

119

park level and later in the Regional Office. Former Lassen Assistant Superintendent Lew Albert came from a ranching family which raised horses, and he was
an avid rider himself. He thus knew Lassen well and also how to pass along the
right information to the right people in NPS. When I asked Mr. Albert about the
contradiction between using horses inside the Park and the purpose of wilderness legislation and planning, he simply replied that the horse had long been
used in the Park, that it does "very little" damage to the environment, and that
it was a popular animal. His response was a typical example of the seat-of-the-
pants management style prevalent among some NPS bureaucrats whose personal
preferences overrode both legal provisions and scientific method. Some of Albert's
horse-riding friends have lobbied hard to have the Lassen superintendent relax
the restrictions. They have on occasion violated the wilderness restrictions on
horses (bringing in twice as many as authorized, straying from trails, tromping in
the fragile mountain meadows, depositing dung in streams, etc.)

Many other requirements and provisions for scientific monitoring of the management plan faced the park staff with an almost insurmountable task from a
manpower standpoint, and also in regard to statistical and technical methods
needed to carry out all the work implied. Again, as in the past, the financial
provisions for Lassen were far below what the plans specified for compliance.
The age-old gap persisted between park-level management, on site, and bureaucrats and politicians responsible for funding and allocation, who like to sit
comfortably in the loges and watch the scenes in the fiefs they oversee.

Toward the end of the seventies, with a Natural Resources Specialist on board,
Lassen's staff strengthened still further its orientation toward scientific decision-
making and management. The federal requirement of an "Environmental Impact Statement" (EIS) to accompany all resource and management plans at park
level had the effect of raising the quality and specificity of planning work. By 1980,
staff had redrafted its original resource management plan, focusing more closely
on issues fundamental to preservation and scientific method:

1) preservation of all evidences of volcanic activity
2) carrying out natural resources research projects
3) utilizing scientific data in decision-making processes
4) managing earth's natural forces of fire, insects, and plant diseases as
   "natural controlling agents" in the park's ecosystems
5) restoring and maintaining acquatic ecosystems in their natural state,
   allowing limited sport fishing so as not to interfere with natural processes

For the first time in natural resource planning, the natural agents of ecological balance, or equilibrium, were recognized as legitimate means for controlling changes in the natural world. These methods, under a very different life style, had been part of the Native Americans' cultural attitude before the impacts of white settlers. It had required over a century for the European-American to reach a similar point of view! In more recent times, another scientific approach utilizing nature's own resources more intelligently and economically, has been developed and proved effective: "Holistic Resource Management." (See Notes.)

But Lassen Park's knowledge base remained still quite deficient for operating by the new standards. The only scientific treatise that addressed the new requirements directly was a study of vascular plants, a complete flower list and an herbarium representing all known plants in the Park. Mammals, aquatics, fowl, and other vegetative species were not yet thoroughly researched or inventoried. These tasks would have to be accomplished if the plan's management recommendations were to be fulfilled. It classified park resources into three broad categories for the purpose of scientific control: terrestrial ecosystems, aquatic ecosystems, and visitor uses.

This approach discarded the old method of attacking "problems" that arose to require attention (For example, "The deer herd is too numerous," hence a new "problem".) Rather it treated each category of life systems (on land, in water and in the air) as interconnecting wholes, each sub-category having influence and significance for the others. Priority would be given to those biotic communities "experiencing ... man-induced alterations." This focus could include impacts of horseriders and horses, from Mr. Albert's equestrian associates on the streams, meadows, and trails in the wilderness areas where they loved to romp. Some non-indigenous vegetation came from undigested seeds in the horses' excrement, seeds from the Sacramento Valley and elsewhere. There were twenty-three known exogenous plants in the Park around 1980, competing for soil, water and sunlight with the Park's own original plant life. But if the park superintendent chose not to accept scientific criteria as a means for finding out the status of ecosystems in his region, then his staff could hardly carry out its lawful mission. Unless they appealed over his head or outside advocacy groups "blew the whistle" on him.

In line with the Federal "Clean Air Act," the Park became responsible for sampling the air quality, which had become suspect due to heavy carbon emissions from automobile traffic in the valley and foothills. Westerly winds carried pollutants into the mountain ranges. This project was budgeted for only three years, however, and thereafter no monitoring would be possible.

In 1984 and again in 1987, the Park's overall plan, now termed the General Management Plan (GMP), received upgrading. Resource Manager Denniston laid out a five-year plan (1984-89) for equipping the Park with the knowledge base, statistical methodology, and personnel equal to the new emphases on scientific management. He identified twenty-six research projects deemed essential for this broad goal. Some projects would be carried out by park staff, as available, and others would be farmed out to other institutions with the appropriate research capability, such as The University of California at Davis, or Humboldt State University. These projects fell into the following categories:

Beaver census
Deer herds
Bear management
Air quality
Geothermal impacts

While these projects fell short of what was needed to monitor all ecosystems, they represented what appeared at the time to be highest priority. About a third of the funds needed for these projects was covered in the park budget, while two-thirds were requested as special monies to come from the Regional Office. The total outlay mounted to almost $250,000 over a five-year period. For later attention, Denniston identified twenty-one other needed projects, with a combined price tag of another $335,000. Almost 98% of all proposed activities were destined for knowledge development purposes to build that scientific base for sound management which had been mentioned sixty years before by Walker Collins and the NPS Education Committee in 1928-29.

Some NPS officials, those charged with planning the new policy science approach that came with the "return to wilderness" goals, had advised Lassen and other parks during previous years to shape their information systems, reporting and budgeting processes in line with the new objectives. Already in 1973, the Regional Chief Scientist in San Francisco advised superintendents that programs must be designed to correct serious environmental problems, so as to facilitate "equilibrium conditions to be achieved and/or maintained in each area's ... principal ecosystem." Budgetary priorities needed to be adjusted in line with these objectives, and submitted to Regional Office, then to NPS and Congress.

Lassen's requests, however, were frequently not supported "upstairs," as was the case in 1978, Denniston's first budget effort. The lists of natural resource projects approved by the Regional Director for 1978 did not include a single

Lassen proposal! Some improvement occurred in subsequent years, but the comparative thinness of Lassen's research monies, as against other parks (for example, Hawaii Volcanic National Park), reflected a starvation diet. When the NPS Regional Director Stanley Albright (nephew of the late Horace Albright) was asked, why this apparent neglect of Lassen's needs in comparison with Hawaii's, he stated that "some superintendents are more aggressive than others." He failed to mention that he had been to Hawaii several times on "inspection visits," but had never once set foot in Lassen!

In the area of water quality, Lassen did not figure in a list of twenty-one western parks for project funding in 1979. Many of Lassen personnel's inititatives were aborted at some bureaucratic level between Mineral and San Francisco, and San Francisco and Washington. Without expanding its knowledge base and scientific-technical capacity (by appointment of specialists, or by contract), Lassen Park could not hope to participate fairly in the new policy-science approach to management. One area of inquiry that was, however, particularly active was that of collecting natural and cultural specimens in the field. During 1969 - 1977, one hundred and thirty four collector permits were issued by the Park's Chief Naturalist. This figure represents wide scientific interest in Lassen Volcanic National Park by the professional community, nearly all of whom were volunteers.

Notwithstanding the strong orientations from both Washington and San Francisco toward scientific endeavor and retraining of staff accordingly, the actual progress at Lassen in creating the necessary knowledge base was painfully slow. It implied some shifting of human resources at park level to meet the challenge. NPS called on "traditional" rangers to rethink their roles and enter the "new age" through retraining and reassignment. These words were not easily accepted among the rank-and-file. Chief Ranger Albert Schneider at Lassen commented that his troops could not handle the visitor traffic and protection work as it was, let alone losing staff or staff time to another division for new kinds of duties. Ranger Larry Feser said he still has to "chase the Kelly Ranch cows out of the meadows, when I have time." And so it goes at the level of "real" park management after seventy years of trying to protect the boundaries from cattle and horses. We have a good reason to wonder if some Americans really want to understand the purpose and significance of a national park and the requirements of good management.

When the Resource Managment Specialist position became "Chief of the Resource Management Division" at Lassen Park (1983), Denniston also got some assistance by the appointment of two aides for basic research and statistical services. With some interruptions from time to time, this staffing has been fairly consistent in recent years, enabling the Natural Resources Management Division to plug along its way. Still, with rising visitor pressures and the severe cutbacks in Federal funding throughout the eighties and early nineties, the tensions over assignments of park staff and the limited monies for basic research and environmental monitoring have not strengthened Denniston's overall operation. The tendency at both park level and regional level is to yield to the "necessities" of the day and shore up the ranger protection force to deal with human predators.

As a result of all these factors, Lassen Park still does not have a comprehensive program for inventorying all existing biotic communities. We do not know if some species have disappeared or are in decline or increase. Some help has come via external research projects, usually funded by the "Cooperative Parks Studies Unit," an interagency assistance program for park research. This channel and other cooperative ventures have helped Denniston to make progress in some areas: numbers and kinds of fungi communities (though incomplete), eighty-two wildflower species (incomplete), birds and mammals (both also incomplete) and aquatic and reptilian species (also incomplete). The Park's herbaria collection (stuck in a basement vault) has sixty-one speciments, but is also not a thorough coverage. Scientists at the University of California-Davis confirmed this information and are cooperating with the Park to improve the collection of data in all these areas. This situation existed in 1991 but possibly could have since improved.

Even so, the resources management staff have been able to make sound tentative decisions about living organisms in the Park, their status and needed research. In a recent report, the Division listed twenty-one project areas that ought to be addressed, including: impacts of both native and non-native animals, threatened and endangered species, loss of certain plants, loss of cultural resources, disruption of riparian/coastal dynamics, resources disruption from mineral/geothermal exploration, water degradation, urbanization/development impacts on park resources generally, visibility impairment from air pollution, resource losses due to both consumptive and non-consumptive activities (game-fish sports, poaching, grazing, mining), natural fire regimens, etc.

In 1988, out of twenty-one identified project areas, eleven were being funded from one source or another. A few new projects were added the following year, making a total of fourteen out of twenty-six being funded. Among well informed park specialists and cooperating scientists, this level of activity reflected some recovery of Lassen's science effort from the early eighties, when then USDI Secretary James Watt's policies seriously jeopardized science research efforts in

America's national parks. Watt's subsequent lucrative consultant work in urban real estate ventures reflects the attitude with which he approached preservation issues in his department. In spite of such behavior by Watt and others, career officers like Resources Management Chief Denniston persevere in their mission, whose ideal goal is "to determine in considerable detail what constitutes [a] park's natural systems and how they function." After seventy-five years of service, park managers are now a little closer to knowing what still lives in Lassen Park. Had the aboriginal Native Americans' knowledge been fully appreciated and recorded, they could well have come much closer, much sooner.

Managing with and without Scientific Data: The Manzanita Lake Fiasco

With visitor use mounting steadily throughout the sixties and early seventies, park management was at pains to deliver quality services and to protect the park from over kill. The fact that Lassen did not benefit much from Mission 66 meant that its status-quo facilities and staff complements had to stretch every ounce of energy to meet demands. There was little time for implementing a scientific approach to decision-making or to management tasks in general. Except for one critical area: geological hazards.

Manzanita Lake and its sister lake, Reflection, had been formed by an avalanche of volcanic rock hundreds of years earlier which dammed up the creek, forming an "alpine lake." Such natural phenomena are common in geological history and reflect the earth's normal evolution. In the process ecological equilibrium is restored, over time, through natural, adaptive processes. The result at Manzanita Lake was one of those non-replicable sylvan settings which has for generations earned the admiration of all who visit the site. It has been aptly described as a "mountain jewel that [became] the lodestone for visitors." Surrounded on all shores by graceful evergreens interspersed with Aspens which radiate their golden leaves in the Fall, and shining resplendently under bright blue summer skies, Manzanita Lake offers the lover of scenic nature a feast of delicate tones and forms which could never be duplicated by human hands. No wonder than that Manzanita Lake was Lassen's prized visiting and camping area. No wonder the Atsugewi Indians adored their native land.

But what about geological hazard? Since the 1920s, geologists had studied Lassen's volcanism and geological events that created the present range and its many unusual features. From time to time, new research efforts were launched which shed more light on them. Such was the case in the sixties, when the U.S.

125

Geological Survey assigned a project to two geologists, Dwight R. Crandell and Donal (sic) R. Mullineaux. This work responded to NPS policy on scientific information for park management. Dr. Howell Williams of the University of California-Berkeley had focused some attention on the avalanche theory in his early work and shed light on the relationship between the mountain's "Chaos Crags," a large volcanic up-cropping on Lassen's north slope, and the geography of the Manzanita Lake area. He described the approximate mass of material, perhaps 70 - 80% of the original formation, that had avalanched down slope and across the flat area ending at Manzanita Creek. (See Notes for references.)

It was in this "end-point" area, and slightly behind a ridge adjacent to the avalanche's original path, that Manzanita Lake facilities were concentrated: the Park's largest campground, its only amphitheatre for program presentations, concessioner's motel-restaurant-store-gas station complex, the Loomis Museum, park naturalist's residence and other amenities. In one sense, this site was the heart and soul of Lassen Volcanic National Park. Much dedication and emotion were tied up with this combination of history, services and culture. Manzanita Lake was the park Cinderella at Lassen, a special spot for vacationers, romantics, fishermen, scientists and just about anyone who was "serious" about visiting Lassen. The one thing among many that they truly missed most in their alpine adventure was a true Visitors Center where they could enjoy an overview of the Park, reference materials, gifts and books for sale and audio-visual facilities. The Museum had proved, for over thirty years, to be inadequate and limited. Super-intendents and park naturalists had appealed over and over again to the NPS hierarachy to invest in a decent, functional facility.

A spectre began to haunt this forest idyll and cast a foreboding shadow over its future as a tourist haven. Crandell and Mullineaux published their report, first as an administrative document (1970), and later in a geological journal (1974). With little or no reference to the question of the amount of mass loss from Chaos Crags from the earlier avalanches, they in so many words declared that the path of any future avalanche endangered the entire Manzanita area. They did not issue a warning to vacate the area, but simply stated that no future development ought to occur there and that an administrative decision was warranted about what parts of the facilities should be removed or displaced so as to be beyond reasonable danger.

I have not been able to ascertain the bases for the original decision, motive, or reason for these geologists' initiating their research at the time they did, that is around 1966-67. It was the end of Mission 66, a major disappointment to

Lassen's superintendents and staff. They minced no words in telling both the Regional Office and NPS-Washington that Lassen had been severely short-changed and mistreated, once again. I can only surmise that hard feelings were certainly in the air. I can also say, based on some of the stories already told in this book, that Lassen Park had received more than its share of bad deals over the decades. It looked as if another bad deal was in the making. NPS officials seemed inclined again to apply the brakes to further development.

Much of this corner of the Park and Manzanita Lake facilities in particular actually lay on top of an avalanche-rock mass one hundred feet or more thick. That mass, popularly called "Chaos Jumbles," represented at least 70% of what had once made up the Chaos Crags mass. The question for park management was, "What is the geological likelihood of a repeat of that avalanche force and volume descending onto the Manzanita Lake landscape and threatening life and property?" This question would have been the kind to elicit all available scientific evidence bearing on that likelihood. The nature of the inquiry and much dialog among park, community and NPS officialdom took a rather different course.

First, the character of and possible threat of Chaos Crags were known from the late 1920s in the work of geologists Williams and Finch. Geologist Crandell had worked in the area during 1955-57 and was very familiar with the geology and problems posed by avalanche material. Their studies indicated no imminent menace to park operations. Was there anything really new in the Geological Survey report of 1970? Apparently not, if other non-governmental studies as well as government data are given equal and fair hearing.

The limits of the huge rock transfers lay just at the outskirts of most visitor use facilities. The wording in the Crandell-Mullineaux report was cautious, avoiding terms such as imminent danger or threats to life and property. But they did advise against large-scale development in the path of some ultimate second occurrence of a massive avalanche. The decision, they wrote, is an administrative one, not a geologically dictated one. However, the NPS Geologist, Robert H. Rose, took an alarmist stance on the Crandell report and, in the arbitrary style of previous NPS decisions, called for complete removal of all park facilities! But one of the Park's staff, Chief Park Naturalist Richard Vance, was a scientist in his own right and searched for more evidence. After reviewing all the relevant data, extensive study of the site itself and consulting with geologist Crandell personnally, Vance came to the conclusion that Manzanita Lake did not lie in direct danger or in the path of some future rock slide. His assistant Park Naturalist, Henry Warren, participated in this work and came to the same conclusion, which was recorded in an official memorandum to the NPS Director, Howard Chapman.

On receiving this information, Chapman reportedly telephoned Vance to tell him that the memorandum was "poppycock" and he would hear none of it. Commenting on this episode some years later, Vance said that it was one of the weirdest telephone conversations he had ever had: "The man simply would not see reason or consider any evidence that contradicted his opinion. It's as if he had already made up his mind and refused to budge." At higher NPS levels it appeared that Chapman's viewpoint held firm and that plans to shut down all Manzanita operations were underway. Washington officials did not counter his recommendation, and so one of the National Park Service's most interesting natural beauties, a valuable and treasured spot in the Park, faced annihilation apparently because of a questionable interpretation of scientific information about a geological problem. This kind of geological condition was certainly not uncommon throughout the Western region of the U.S., Hawaii and Alaska, where volcanic and other geological hazards are a way of life for park management.

Lassen's superintendents during this period (1970 - 74), Richard Boyer and Robert Murphy, were both shocked and appalled at the strange position taken by their superiors. Their efforts to reinterpret the data and to find alternatives to complete shutdown fell on deaf ears. Murphy even went over Chapman's head to NPS-Washington to plead his case on "hands and knees," but was categorically rebuffed. Somehow all doors were closed, and there seemed to be no way out of the impasse. In an interview, Murphy said that "they had made up their minds before all the evidence was in, or before any serious alternative to Lassen's visitor and educational needs was considered." Although he was aware of and participated in NPS discussions of some other arrangements in the general Manzanita Lake area, and about other plans for the Park, he saw through the ongoing discussions as window dressing, and remained pessimistic. Soon thereafter, Murphy asked for a transfer out. Another loss for Lassen and the community.

Another viewpoint on this matter needs to be aired: that the primary objective of the closure aimed to satisfy the environmentalists and the "purists" in the NPS. The champion of this interpretation was Don Hummel, former Lassen Park Ranger and the first concessioner in the Park at Manzanita Lake. Obviously, Don Hummel's emotions were aroused by Chapman's decision and that of NPS Director Ron Walker. In view of the data which this story has just presented, and my intimate knowledge of the relevant files and interviews with the main participants in the affair, Hummel's accusations carry little if any weight. Don Hummel's legal background (law degree from The University of Michigan) and lack of scientific expertise about Lassen's ecosystems, together with his long political career, raise questions about the kinds of allegations he makes in his book, "Stealing the National Parks." Environmentalists certainly advocated preservation of wilderness areas like Lassen and opposed over-use by non-discriminating visitors. Lassen's natural conditions were in fact threatened, and its return to its once primitive state, as required by law, remained at best a "long shot." Here, Hummel seems well off target.

Later the views of Lassen park specialists, such as Vance and Henry Warren, were vindicated. At the request of businessman John Koeberer of Red Bluff, the engineering firm of Woodward-Clyde Consultants was asked to look at the geological features of Chaos Crags and vicinity. After reviewing all the literature and conducting field visits, that firms' conclusions ran squarely against Chapman's position. Their report stated that "the conditions which produced [avalanches] are no longer present." The massive rock walls and the once low valley lying before Manzanita Lake are gone, the first having filled the second. "The presence of the debris material ... has reduced the elevation that would be available for an air-borne avalanche..." Furthermore, the rock avalanche of three hundred years or so ago "appears to be a unique event, and ... has reduced the potential for a similarly large event from that location in the future." Any future rockfall, these geologists estimated, would be quite small and far from capable of reaching Manzanita Lake. In response one can say that in this geologically complex earth anything is possible, but this caveat is applicable to many other national parks, Lassen being only one among many having volcanic and earthquake-prone forces in its makeup.

This information came too late, however, to reverse Director Chapman's verdict: "Close it down!" But there was another fly in the Manzanita Lake ointment: the future of the private concessioner at Manzanita Lake, Terrence Cullinan, President of the Lassen Volcanic National Park Company (Menlo Park, CA). In consultations with park officials, he expressed the hope that the geological report, which he termed "speculative," would not lead to either a halt in future development or to curtailment of present operations. In much memo-writing and discussion back and forth, he got wind that Chapman's course led to dead end, and closure. He then raised the matter of compensation. At the same time, the Manzanita Lodge and other tourist facilities were then operating at only 50% capacity. This situation was partly due to the swing in visitor preferences toward more wilderness-type and environmental kinds of contact, which reached all-time highs in the late sixties and early seventies. In line with this factor was the Company's delay in both upgrading and expanding its services. Although Cullinan at first viewed Chapman's postion in a negative way, later he changed his mind and became favorably inclined toward closure based on the geological hazards argument. Chapman would be faced with making compensation to the company in the event of closure, or of further delay of a decision on expanding park facilities.

The closure scenario apparently appealed most to Chapman, who wanted to avoid judicial proceedings and perhaps even higher costs, inasmuch as NPS continued, even before the geological issue, to repress Lassen's development initiatives. All the while, discussions among park managers, NPS officials, and community representatives proceeded on the Lassen master plan. In pouring over all the reams of memoranda, draft reports, preliminary plans, and technical opinions, I could not avoid the conclusion that most of these discussions were sterile and plain message chaff. There would really be no development of significance at Lassen, just as in the past. It was a remote place without significant influence at levels of serious political discussions. With one exception: Congressman H. T. "Bizz" Johnson. While Johnson stood pretty much alone in his lobbying for Lassen, his efforts focussed on one objective, the ski concession. Why? He was pressured by the sports groups and commercial ski interests to get approval for an expanded and up-to-date ski facility, replete with triple-chair lifts and the rest. Red Bluff ski operator John Koeberer pressed Johnson to have NPS approve major expansion of his facilities. His effort to refute the rock avalanche theory improved his rapport with the park superintendent and staff.

One of the NPS engineers assigned to Lassen projects, Kenneth Raithel, was lobbied by Bizz Johnson about the ski plans and passed the information on to his superiors. Johnson's votes on other issues of NPS interest were bargaining chips in favor of the ski concession. Although his record is one of verbally seeking a solution to Lassen's difficult situation, in the final analysis it appeared to be a finesse aimed at achieving other, more limited objectives for some of his supporting constituents. So at the highest levels, policy making continued in the tradition of ignoring vital data essential to sound ecological management.

When the concessioner appealed on April 5, 1974 to the Interior Secretary for a quick decision on his operation, NPS was ordered to condemn the area as unsafe and one which the Government would not agree to protect. Cullinan's economic motive was the one which really forced Chapman to act quickly. He immediately put out his diktat in a telegram dated April 26, 1974. He did not even bother to telephone or to meet with Superintendent Bob Murphy, or to consult further with staff. It was another one of those Harold Ickes type blows. Shortly thereafter, Bob Murphy packed his bags as had Boyer before him.

The NPS decisions on Manzanita Lake did reserve one piece of the pie: parts of the magnificent campground, believed by pro-NPS geologists to be out of range of an avalanche, would be retained and reopened at a future date. But in the interim, the whole complex of facilities, with all their historical and cultural meaning for Fire Mountain, stopped dead in their tracks. Deep sleep fell over Lassen, such as it had not seen since Walker Collins in 1935 got the order from Washington to vacate his precious seat. NPS and the Interior Department repeated their arbitrary pattern of control.

But there were winners, at least one: Congressman Johnson got his promise from Chapman that a new ski operation was in the works. Cullinan's park concession company received a large pay-off from Uncle Sam and left the area. Was he a winner too? And Howard Chapman kept his job. Lassen Park would be able to auction off or rehabilitate whatever the company left behind after pocketing the cash. All the players in this incredible game were at the decision-making table when Lassen's fate was decided, except the Superintendent of Lassen Volcanic National Park: he had gone over the hill. He was replaced by the park maintenance chief at Yosemite, Bill Stephenson, a career maintenance man with limited management experience.

For years, even decades, after the traumatic events of 1969-1974, park employees and park supporters discussed and rehashed the events and decisions time and again. Emotions ran high, and the fact that no truly representative participation either by park staff as a whole, or by community constituents, in the deliberations leading to Director Chapman's decision, had taken place, helped to raise suspicions and doubts about the entire proceedings. To this date, the "Manzanita Lake Affair" brings bitterness and recriminatory remarks by many who love the "Lands of Lassen." The character and quality of decision-making also revealed a notable lack of due process and respect for professional values in NPS. Some officials simply ignored their park-level experts, rode herd over all dissenting opinions, and let the chips fall where they may. According to many who observed these events first-hand , NPS leaders failed to protect Lassen Park's basic interests. This brand of management is now a matter of record.

My own experience in government and similar kinds of bureaucracies, leads me to conclude that these well positioned players with the public wealth pursued interests other than defense of the Park. Otherwise, what incentives did they have to behave in the fashion that they did? Their saving grace was, that there are no real checks and balances to their behaviors, especially when those behaviors are protected by political superiors. A host of bureaucratic scandals in both legislative and executive branches of government in the past fifteen years lends plausibility to such a viewpoint.

The nature of political behavior seeks both protection of one's position and gaining support from as broad a spectrum as possible. The kinds of bargaining, favors and denials referred to here can explain some of the negative treatments which Lassen Park received at the hands of a number of regional directors. In Mr. Chapman's case, when he was asked some leading questions about the Park's poor standing and unmet needs as compared to other parks, he put down in writing his views on the subject. The following are summaries of his replies, along with the my own comment on them.

1. Lassen's under-funding was primarily due to a lack of political interest and pressures at the state and federal levels. [Comment: Largely inaccurate. Beginning with Congressman Raker, and then Congressmen Engle, Englebright, Johnson, Heger and Fazio, there has been strong support for Lassen. However, NPS officials either yielded in favor of other budget demands, or traded off certain projects, such as ski lifts, for support by the politicians on other items. State agencies and the communities have also maintained strong support down the years. As for aggressiveness of Lassen superintendents, there were many examples of outstanding performance by Lassen's superintendents: Collins, Preston, Hallock, Boyer, and Murphy, to name a few of the "table-pounding" men who faced up to NPS officials, but with precious little success.]

2. Visitor uses of Lassen did not compare well with those of other parks, a factor which always put it at lower priorities for funding. [Misleading statement. Given Lassen's small size of 106,000 acres, visitor uses have since the mid-sixties varied between 400,000 and 600,000. To compare these figures with two jewels of the park service, Yosemite (with 760,000 acres), and Yellowstone (with 2.1 million acres), the first would have to reach seven times Lassen's rate of use, while the second twenty times. Neither of those two parks have equalled Lassen's visitor intensity in terms of size.]

3. Lassen is too remote from metropolitan areas and distance does not favor it in terms of visibility. [Strange statement. Is Yellowstone or Grand Tetons within easy metropolitan range? How about Bryce Canyon, or Big Bend? The director's geography seems weak on this point.]

4. At the time of the 1981 GMP go-rounds, the Federal budget was undergoing heavy cutting, reducing Lassen's chances of receiving its due. [Partially correct. But other parks faced the same dilemma, and when we compare what Lassen got, with what Hawaii Volcanic National Park got, Lassen was definitely on the short end of the stick.]

132

5. Delays were caused by administrative and bureacratic red-tape, and Lassen's requests just got jam-logged. [Weak alibi. Federal red-tape faces every park, big and small, and the fact is that most parks were treated fairly while Lassen took a back seat.]

6. Lassen's geological hazards were uncommon in the park system and negated its chances for better consideration. [Misleading statement. Many parks have hazards not unlike those at Lassen, both volcanic and non-volcanic in nature. But they are not penalized because of their geology. Furthermore, Chapman flatly rejected alternative arguments that refuted his position. Partial proof of his spurious reasoning is the fact that, once the Manzanita Lake concession had been bought out, he approved a couple years later reopening the campgrounds there.]

That's the official explanation for Lassen's long drought. But the documentation presented in this story etches a different one.

The Manzanita Lake Affair played itself out in a fashion consistent with all the other crises and issues that over the years have blighted Lassen Park's glow in the galaxy of national parks. Somewhat as in the "twelve million dollar hole" scenario, top managers glossed over the legal print, ignored advice from those in charge at park level, misused scientific data and made momentous decisions affecting tens of thousands of citizens on the basis of their personal preferences. Little wonder that many park visitors and users feel justified in flouting official park rules by saying, with indignation, "This here is our park and we'll do what we darn well please."

Also, it demonstrates that it is not enough to espouse philosophies about our natural and cultural heritage; it is not enough even to pass laws to implement a policy or commitment; it is not sufficient to staff parks with well trained professionals, if those who are in charge and those who actually access the parks do not imbibe the spirit and intent of those laws and its implementers. Herein lies the major challenge to the future of parks like Lassen Volcanic National Park, that bright gem crowning the Cascade Mountains at the end of their trail, that great Fire Mountain which our Native American forebearers cherished as their homeland but lost in their battle with the "civilizers" from the East. Their spirits are still there, watching over the new custodians and their wiles. If we in the future become even half committed to restoring the Lands of Lassen to pre-settler conditions, perhaps the Great Spirit will once again bless those Lands with the harmony and viability they once had in their primitive state. But time may not be on our side.

AN EPILOGUE

Over the past one hundred and fifty years in northeastern California, European-Americans have succeeded in annihilating aboriginal cultures in the region of Lassen Volcanic National Park. They supplanted natural ecological systems, with which previous Indian societies had maintained a perpetual equilibrium for thousands of years, with man-made constructs based on large-scale exploitation of natural resources. This wholescale transformation, which took place under the banner of the "stars and stripes" and the motto "Manifest Destiny," changed forever the conditions in which nature and man would coexist. Eventually, the foreign settlers were themselves replaced in part by the U.S. Government, which installed public management of those natural ecosystems in hopes of preserving them for future generations. In one sense, government officials supplanted in turn the white settlers as managers of forests and wilderness areas.

The story of these developments is an odyssey in miniature of humans' sojourn on this earth of ours. It reveals, in a particular natural context, how human beings have chosen to interact with the planet's original endowments. The scenarios which etch the impacts of people on once primeval lands show how radically different human attitudes toward nature expressed the values and behaviors of those in control of the land.

The story is also a kind of elusive search for a quality of life. The search follows a path from "primitive," to "exploited," to "protected," to "educational-recreational," and now apparently back to "primitive," all in the space of a century of human endeavors. The path has hardly ever been direct or clear, and it has made abrupt turns, flipped backwards, or simply marked time when national preserves suffered from neglect. After a rather brilliant beginning under its first superintendent, Walker Collins, Lassen Volcanic National Park continually felt the pangs of neglect because of political issues, petty intrigues and insensitivities to its mission. Its staff never had a fair opportunity to demonstrate to the visiting public their full vision of a quality of life far from congested, urban scenes in our increasingly forbidden cities.

Evidence in the Lassen experience suggests that the parks are failing in their mission as orginally defined in 1916, and as projected by the noble aspirations of

134

early leaders of the National Park Service (NPS). At a time when earth's life-sustaining systems are under jeopardy from man-made elements, the educational portent and example of natural ecologies, which parks and similar preserves represent, take on ever more significance for human society. But how can we measure the accomplishments of a national park system dedicated to those principles? Lassen Park is a good case for testing out the commitments made to the American people almost a century ago.

This story bears out that our methods for preserving the Nation's natural and cultural heritage still leave much to be done, in terms of civic-mindedness, ecological wholeness, and scientific management. Principled leadership, skilled and dedicated managers and well-informed, if not enlightened, users of our parks are essential ingredients to a new era in our national preservation movement. If the past is indeed prologue to what comes after, we need yet to learn much from our Native American forbearers, from the mistakes of the early settlers and from our park managers' records. We have the knowledge to change our ways, but do we have the will and the time?

We now know the rest of the stories that only faintly get mention in the school books, on the fate of our Indian tribes and on the ravages perpetrated on their primeval lands. We know the stakes that were set for the control over their territory, and how its rapid degradation finally led to a revision of public policy. It's up to the younger generation now ascending to positions of leadership to implement that policy in both the spirit and the letter of its original intent.

At this point in human culture, it is imperative that people begin to understand that our greatest challenge for survival lies in designing a healthy, benign and functional interdependency with our natural endowments. Urban cultures can no longer function without regard to the conditions of their outlying ecosystems, to which they are naturally related in a seamless web of life. To rehabilitate human civilization requires constant and patient efforts by all our institutions along paths suggested by this story. The direction we must go is clear, and we can trust in Ishi's simple but profound observation, "Nature is always true."

NOTES

Chapter 1. For details on Lassen area geology, consult P. Kane (1980), P. Schultz (1959), and H. Williams (1932). A general treatise on ecology is Allen Savory (1988).

Descriptions of Native American cultures are based on S. Cook (1976), D. Eargle (1989), J. Forbes (1982), T. Garth (1944) and (1953), R. Heizer (1970), R. Heizer and T. Kroeber (1981), A. Kroeber (1925), T. Kroeber (1969), J. Maxwell (1994), P. Schultz (1988), The American Experience (1992), and R. Underhill (1972).

Yana-Yahi villages are depicted in detail by T. Kroeber.

Chapter 2. Sources of information on European-American settlers' impacts are S. Cook (1976), D. Eargle (1989), J. Forbes (1982), A. Kroeber (1974), T. Kroeber (1969), P. Kurtz (1963), J. Maxwell (1994), P. Schultz (1988), J. Sinnott (1976), D. Strong (1982), R. Swartzlow (1982), and The American Experience (1992).

Discussions of conservation and preservation viewpoints are in S. Hays (1975) and S. Fox (1981).

For events leading up to Lassen Park's creation, see W. Medlin (1991) and D. Strong (1982).

Chapter 3. NPS policies and Lassen Park's early development are described in A. Albright (1985) and 1987), S. Fox (1981), W. Medlin (1991), R. Sifford, and D. Strong (1982). Interviews with old timers were also used. National Archives RG-79, LVNP series, were used extensively for this and all subsequent chapters.

Chapter 4. For backgrounds and analyses of conflicting attitudes on national park policies, consult H. Albright (1985) and (1987), S. Fox (1981), S. Hays (1975), J. McClintock (1994), W. Medlin (1991) and F. Tilden (1982).

Chapter 5. Sources for park educational services and relevant background materials are H. Albright (1987), S. Fox (1981), J. Ise (1961), T. Kroeber (1969), W. Medlin (1991), NPS/USDI Administrative Manual (1959), NPS/USDI Historical Listings (1986), Schultz (1988), and D. Strong (1973).

During 1993-94 a modest sum became available, mainly through private grants, to refurbish the dilapidated Museum sufficiently to reopen it to the public.

Chapter 6. Issues of park management are discussed in the American Forester (1969), S. Fox (1981), W. Medlin (1991), National Parks for the 21st Century, The Vail Agenda (1993), NPS/USDI Administrative Manual (1959), A. Savory (1988),D. Strong (1982), F. Tilden (1982), and C. Wirth (1980). The concept of "holistic resource management" is treated at length in A. Savory.

For the controversy over Lassen avalanche threats, and related geological and management issues, consult D. Crandell (1970), D. Eppler (1987), J. Heath (1959), R. Holt (1976), P. Hubbel (1961), D. Hummel (1987), P. Kane (1980), W. Medlin (1991) and H. Williams (1932).

CREDITS

The author acknowledges permissions granted by the following agencies and publishers to reproduce graphics and textual materials over which they have either jurisdiction or copyright.

National Park Service, U.S. Department of Interior: Figures 1-2, 1-3, 2-2, 2-3, 2-4, 3-1, 3-2, 3-4, 4-1, and 5-1.

University of Oklahoma Press: Quotation from Conrad Wirth. *Parks, politics and the people.* (1980).

The Virginia Kidd Literary Agency (Milford, PA): Figures 1-1 and 1-4.

Dolan H. Eargle, Jr. (map) and Julie Nunes (art work), Figure 2-1.

REFERENCES

Abbey, Robert H. "Early day experiences in the U.S. Forest Service," Part I, 1905-1920. (Mimeographed text). 1932.

Albright, Horace M. The National Park Service: The story behind the scenery. Las Vegas, NV: KC Publications, 1987.

Albright, Horace M. The birth of the National Park Service: The founding years, 1913-1933. Salt Lake City: Howe Bros., 1985.

"American experience, The. Ishi, the last Yahi." (Video). Boston: WGHB, 1992.

"American Indians and American Life," in The Annals of the American Academy of Political and Social Science, vol. 311, May, 1957.

Amesbury, Robert H. Nobles Emigrant Trail. Susanville, CA: Lassen Litho, 1967.

Anderson, Robert A. Fighting the Mill Creeks. Chico, CA: The Chico Record Press, 1909.

Barbe, G. Douglas and Thomas C. Fuller. "List of California Herbaria and working collections." Sacramento, CA: Calif. State Dept. of Food and Agriculture, 1987.

Baumhoff, M.A. "An introduction to Yana archeology," in University of California Archeological Survey, No. 40, 1957.

Cook, Sherburne F. The conflict between the California Indian and white civilization. Berkeley/Los Angeles: The University of California Press, 1976.

Cook, Sherburne F. The population of the California Indians, 1769-1970. Berkeley: The University of California Press, 1976.

Cooke, William B. Fungi of Lassen Volcanic National Park; Technical Report No. 21, Cooperative National Park Resources Studies Unit. Davis, CA: The University of California, 1985.

Crandell, Dwight R. and Donal R. Mullineaux. "Potential geologic hazards in Lassen Volcanic National Park, California." USGS Administrative Report for the National Park Service, 1970. [Cf. similar report in U.S. Geological Survey Journal of Research, vol. 2, No.1, 1974]

Diller, J.S. "Geology of the Lassen Peak district," in U.S. Geological Survey, 8th Annual Report, Part I, 1886-1887.

Eargle, Dolan H., Jr. The earth is our mother; a guide to the Indians of California. San Francisco, CA: Trees Company Press, 1986.

Eppler, Dean B., et al. "Rheologic properties and kinematics of the Chaos Jumbles rockfall avalanche," in Journal of Geophysical Research, vol. 92, No. B-5, April 10, 1987.

Field, Donald R. and Gary E. Machlis. The organization and the employee in an era of change. National Park Service and Cooperative Park Studies Unit, 1985.

Finch, R.H. "Lassen Report," Nos. 2-33. Mineral, CA: 1926-1933.

Forbes, Jack D. Native Americans of California and Nevada. Revised ed. Happy Camp, CA: Naturegraph Publications, 1982.

Fox, Stephen. John Muir and his legacy. Boston: Little, Brown and Co., 1981

Frazer, Robert W. Forts of the West. Norman, OK: The University of Oklahoma Press, 1972.

Gankin, Roman. A vegetative study, ski area, Mount Lassen Volcanic National Park. Davis, CA: Ecolabs Associates, 1973.

Garth, Thomas R. "Atsugewi ethnography," in Anthropological Records, The University of California, vol. 14, No. 2, Feb. 1953.

Garth, Thomas R. "Kinship terminology, marriage practices, and behavior toward kin among the Atsugewi," in American Anthropologist, vol. 46, No. 3, July-Sept., 1944.

Hays, Samuel P. Conservation and the gospel of efficiency. New York: Atheneum Press, 1969.

Heath, James P. "Repeated avalanches at Chaos Jumbles," in American Journal of Science, vol. 258, Dec. 1960.

Heizer, Robert F. and Theodora Kroeber, Edd. Ishi the last Yahi, a documentary history. Berkley, CA: University of California Press, 1981.

Heizer, R. F. and M.A. Whipple, Edd. The California Indians; a sourcebook. Berkeley, CA: The University of California Press, 1970.

Hill, Dorothy J. Maidu use of native flora and fauna. (Typed MS, 1972.

Hill, Dorothy J. The Indians of Chico Rancheria. Sacramento: California State Dept. of Parks and Recreation, 1978.

Holt, Robert G. "Lassen's silent threat," in National Parks and Recreation Magazine, vol. 30, No. 6, June, 1978.

Hubbell, Paul M. A survey of Manzanita and Reflection Lakes, Lassen Volcanic National Park. Arcata, CA: Humboldt State College, 1961.

Hummel, Don. Stealing the national parks. Bellevue, WA: Merril Press, 1987.

Ise, John. Our national park policy. Baltimore: The Johns Hopkins University Press, 1961.

Journey, Alfred E. "An Archeological survey of Lassen Volcanic National Park." Master of Arts thesis, California State University at Sacramento, 1975.

Kane, Phillip S. Through Vulcan's eye; the geology and morphology of Lassen Volcanic National Park, California." Red Bluff, CA: Walker Lithograph, Inc., 1980.

Kroeber, Alfred L. "Basic report on California Indian land holdings; selected writings on land use and political organization of California Indians," in California Indians, IV, David A. Horr, Ed. American Indian Ethnography. New York: Garland Publishing Co., 1974.

Kroeber, Theodora. Ishi in two worlds; a biography of the last wild Indian in North America. Berkeley/Los Angeles: The University of California Press, 1969.

Kurtz, Patricia L. A history of Indian Valley, Plumas County, California, 1850-1920. Master of Arts thesis, Chico State University, 1963.

Leopold, Aldo Starker. "Wildlife management in the national parks ["The Leopold Report"]. U.S. Dept. of Interior; typed MS. March, 1963. (Reprinted in, The American Forester, vol. 69, No. 4)

Long, Norton E. The polity. Chicago: Rand McNally, 1962.

Maclean, Norman. A river runs through it. Chicago: The University of Chicago Press, 1983.

Maxwell, James A., Ed. America's fascinating Indian heritage. Pleasantville, NY: The Reader's Digest Association, 1994.

McClintock, James J. Nature's kindred spirits. Madison, WI: The University of Wisconsin Press, 1994.

Medlin, William K. "A model for planning rural education development," in Convergence (Toronto), vol. 16, No. 2, 1983.

Medlin, William K. Vulcan's triumph: The history of Lassen Volcanic National Park under human management. An administrative history. Mineral, CA: Loomis Museum Association, 1991.

Milne, Robert C. Birds of Lassen Volcanic National Park. Mineral, CA: Loomis Museum Association, 1966.

Nelson, Raymond L. Trees and shrubs of Lassen Volcanic National Park. Mineral, CA: Loomis Museum Association, 1971.

Purdy, Tim I. Sixty years of Siffords at Drakesbad. Susanville, CA: Lahonton Images, 1994.

Richard, Ellis. Lassen Volcanic, the story behind the scenery. Las Vegas, NV: KC Publications, 1988.

Runte, Alfred. National Parks; the American experience. Lincoln, NE: The University of Nebraska Press, 1987.

Sapir, Edward and Leslie Spier. "Notes on the culture of the Yana," in Anthropological Records, vol. 3, No. 3, 1943.

Savory, Allen. Holistic resource management. Washington, DC: Island Press, 1988.

Schultz, Paul E. Geology of Lassen's landscape. Mineral, CA: Loomis Museum Association, 1959.

Schultz, Paul E. Indians of Lassen Volcanic National Park and vicinity. Mineral, CA: Loomis Museum Association, 1988.

Shankland, Robert. Steve Mather of the national parks. New York: Alfred A. Knopf, 1951.

Sierra Club Outing Committee. A report on the wilderness impact study. Palo Alto, CA: Consolidated Publications, 1977.

Sinnott, James J. History of Sierra County, vol. IV, Sierra Valley. Pioneer, CA: The California Traveler, Inc., 1976.

Smith, Anthony W. Preserving wilderness in our national parks. Washington, DC: National Parks and Conservation Association, 1971.

Strong, Douglas H. These happy grounds; a history of the Lassen region. Red Bluff: Walker Lithograph Co., 1973.

Swain, Donald C. Wilderness defender, Horace M. Albright and conservation. Chicago: The University of Chicago Press, 1970.

Swartzlow, Ruby J. Lassen, his life and legacy. Mineral, CA: Loomis Museum Association, 1964.

Tilden, Freeman. The national parks. New York: Alfred A. Knopf, 1970.

Underhill, Ruth M. Red man's religion. Chicago: The University of Chicago Press, 1972.

U.S. Department of Interior, National Park Service. Administrative Manual/ Handbook. 1952, 1955, 1959, and 1964.

U.S. Department of Interior and National Resources Board. "Recreational use of land in the United States. Washington, DC: GPO, 1938.

Vail Agenda, The. National Parks for the 21st century. (Report to the Director of the National Park Service). Post Mills, VI: Chelsea Green Publishing Co. (1993?)

Williams, Howell M. "Geology of the Lassen Volcanic National Park, California," in University of California Department of Geology Sciences Bulletin, vol. 12, 1932.

Wirth, Conrad L. Parks, politics and the people. Norman, OK: The University of Oklahoma Press, 1980.

www.ingramcontent.com/pod-product-compliance
Lightning Source LLC
Chambersburg PA
CBHW031435270326

41930CB00007B/725